D1233498

Published by
Walker Publishing Company, Inc., New York
Distributed to the trade by
Holtzbrinck Publishers

Printed on recycled paper.

Library of Congress Cataloging-in-Publication Data
has been applied for.

ISBN-10: 0-8027-1634-2
ISBN-13: 978-0-8027-1634-7

Visit Walker & Company's Web site
at www.walkerbooks.com

First U.S. edition 2007

1 3 5 7 9 10 8 6 4 2

Designed and typeset by
Wooden Books Ltd, Glastonbury, UK

Printed in the United States of America

THE MAYAN
AND OTHER ANCIENT
CALENDARS

Geoff Stray

Walker & Company
New York

WOODEN BOOKS

Much gratitude to my loving mother, Eileen

Thanks to the following for their help with illustrations: Will Spring (p.4, 15, 30), Sven Gronemeyer (p.49), my editor John Martineau (p.37, 39), and Matt Tweed (p.11). Thanks also to Clare Johnson, John Major Jenkins, John Hoopes, and Mike Finley for their contributions and suggestions; any errors remain my own. Pictures and glyphs have been taken and adapted from Biologia Centrali-Americana *by A.P.Maudslay, London 1889-1902,* Vues des Cordilleres et Monuments des Pueples Indigenes de l'Amerique *by A.Humboldt, Paris 1810,* Voyage Pittoresque et Archeologique *by F.Waldeck, Paris 1838,* Report on Teotihuacan *by R.Almaraz, Paris 1866, and Iconographic Encyclopaedia of Science, Literature, and Art, engraved by H. Winkles, New York 1851.*

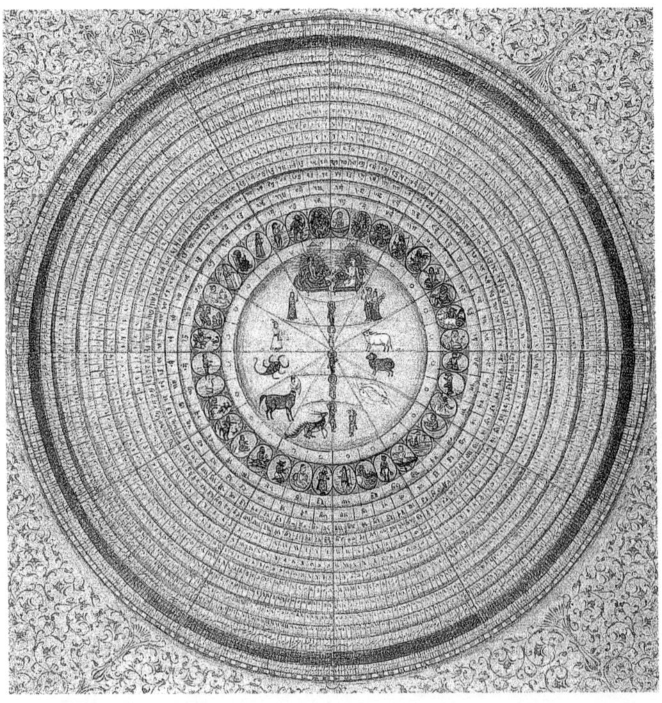

A 19th century Indian zodiac, showing the twelve zodiacal signs, the planetary lords of the 36 decans, and further subdivisions. Adapted from a copy in the British Museum.

CONTENTS

	3114 BC 0.0.0.0.0	2720 BC 1.0.0.0.0	2325 BC 2.0.0.0.0	1931 BC 3.0.0.0.0	1537 BC 4.0.0.0.0	1143 BC 5.0.0.0.0	748 BC 6.0.0.0.0	354 BC 7.0.0.0.0	41 AD 8.0.0.0.0	435 AD 9.0.0.0.0	830 AD 10.0.0.0.0	1224 AD 11.0.0.0.0	1618 AD 12.0.0.0.0		
Aug 11th 3114 BC	1	8	2	9	3	10	4	11	5	12	6	13	7	12.0.0.0.0	1618 AD
3094 BC	2	9	3	10	4	11	5	12	6	13	7	1	8	12.1.0.0.0	1638 AD
3074 BC	3	10	4	11	5	12	6	13	7	1	8	2	9	12.2.0.0.0	1658 AD
3055 BC	4	11	5	12	6	13	7	1	8	2	9	3	10	12.3.0.0.0	1677 AD
3035 BC	5	12	6	13	7	1	8	2	9	3	10	4	11	12.4.0.0.0	1697 AD
3015 BC	6	13	7	1	8	2	9	3	10	4	11	5	12	12.5.0.0.0	1717 AD
2996 BC	7	1	8	2	9	3	10	4	11	5	12	6	13	12.6.0.0.0	1736 AD
2976 BC	8	2	9	3	10	4	11	5	12	6	13	7	1	12.7.0.0.0	1756 AD
2956 BC	9	3	10	4	11	5	12	6	13	7	1	8	2	12.8.0.0.0	1776 AD
2936 BC	10	4	11	5	12	6	13	7	1	8	2	9	3	12.9.0.0.0	1796 AD
2917 BC	11	5	12	6	13	7	1	8	2	9	3	10	4	12.10.0.0.0	1815 AD
2897 BC	12	6	13	7	1	8	2	9	3	10	4	11	5	12.11.0.0.0	1835 AD
2877 BC	13	7	1	8	2	9	3	10	4	11	5	12	6	12.12.0.0.0	1855 AD
2858 BC	1	8	2	9	3	10	4	11	5	12	6	13	7	12.13.0.0.0	1874 AD
2838 BC	2	9	3	10	4	11	5	12	6	13	7	1	8	12.14.0.0.0	1894 AD
2818 BC	3	10	4	11	5	12	6	13	7	1	8	2	9	12.15.0.0.0	1914 AD
2798 BC	4	11	5	12	6	13	7	1	8	2	9	3	10	12.16.0.0.0	1934 AD
2779 BC	5	12	6	13	7	1	8	2	9	3	10	4	11	12.17.0.0.0	1953 AD
2759 BC	6	13	7	1	8	2	9	3	10	4	11	5	12	12.18.0.0.0	1973 AD
2739 BC	7	1	8	2	9	3	10	4	11	5	12	6	13	12.19.0.0.0	1993 AD

Last day **Dec 21st 2012**

The fundamental structure of the Maya calendar, showing the 5125-year Long Count mapped onto the 260-day Tzolkin. Each box contains a katun, 20 tuns of 360 days. Each column represents a baktun of 20 katuns. Any four quadrilaterally symmetrical squares (e.g., the four corners) sum to 28. Groups of four containing the mean and extreme numerals 1, 7 and 13 have been shaded (and the central column treated as a special case). The DNA double helix has the same 13:20 proportion. See too page 19 - look carefully!

INTRODUCTION

From the moment mankind learned to count, sow seeds, and form records, attempts were also made to keep track of the sun and the moon. The calendars that subsequently appeared across the planet are of three broad types: *Lunar* calendars follow the phases of the Moon, ignoring the Sun, adding occasional *intercalary* days as corrections. *Luni-solar* calendars have months based on the movement of the moon, (alternating between 29 and 30 days to approximate the 29.5-day lunar cycle), with intercalary months inserted to keep the lunar and solar years from drifting too far away from each other. *Solar* calendars simply track the seasons, intercalating days to keep the calendar in line with the solar year.

In addition to these basic types we may add the *stellar* calendars of antiquity triggered by the *heliacal rising* of a star, and, finally, the most sophisticated calendars of all, those which incorporated the cycles of planets. This last and most extraordinary type is unique in world history to the Maya, and forms the second half of this book.

With interest in the Mayan calendar systems growing, the absence of a handy pocket guide has become increasingly evident. The painstaking work of decoding the few surviving Mayan manuscripts and monuments started in the late 1800s and continues today. Every effort has been made to ensure that the information in this book concurs with the most recent advances in understanding.

At the heart of all calendars is the idea of cycles, and therefore of prediction. I predict you are in for an interesting read.

The Fundamental Cycles

sun, moon, earth, and stars

Shown opposite are some of the natural physical cycles that have been the cause and inspiration of many ancient calendars.

Familiar to all of us today is the basic 365.242-day solar year, (*shown central opposite*). We also recognize the length of time we call a day. If only they meshed easily together! Instead, every four years there are nearly 1461 days, or, better, every 33 years there are almost exactly 12,053 days. It is the tilt of the earth which produces the seasons, and this very slowly rotates over nearly 26,000 years, an event known as the *precession of the equinoxes*, creating a tiny difference between the *sidereal* (star-based) day (and year) and the more familiar *tropical* (seasonal, sun-based) values.

Another obvious cycle is that of lunations, or full moons. At 29.53 days this was the backbone of many ancient calendars. It too does not synchronize easily with the solar year: there are 12.368 full moons in an average year, or roughly 37 full moons in three years. There are, more exactly, 235 lunations in 19 years, this length of time being known as the *Metonic cycle*, after the 5th century BC Greek astronomer Meton. This was subsequently refined into days by Callippus in 330 BC who used four Metonic cycles less one day to give a 76-year cycle of 27,759 days containing 940 lunations.

The tilt of the moon's orbit relative to the sun's passage, or *ecliptic*, produces the two *moon's nodes*, where the paths of the sun and moon cross, the locations of which are vital for eclipse prediction. The nodes rotate slowly every 18.613 years in the opposite direction to the sun, meaning the sun returns to the same node in less than a year, every 346.620079 days, the *Draconic*, or *eclipse year.*

Sidereal Day

23.9344686 hours. *Rotation period of the earth relative to the stars.*

Tropical Day

24 hours. *Rotation period of the earth relative to the sun.*

Precession of Equinoxes

25,920 years (Great Year). *Slow rotation period of the earth's tilt.*

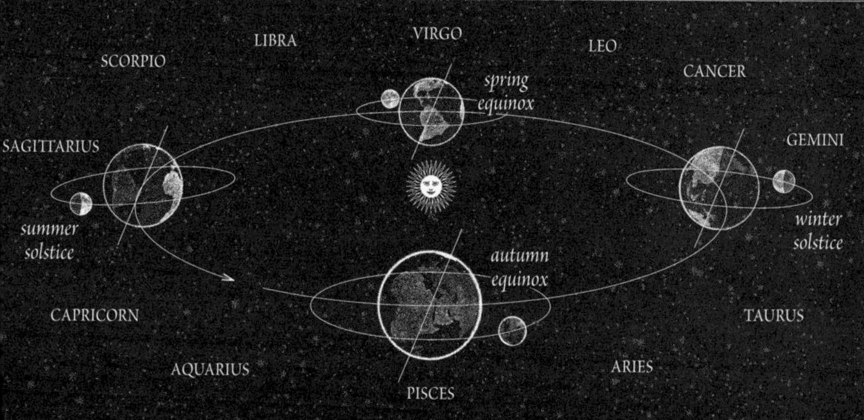

The Tropical Year

365.2421904 days. *The length of time between midsummer or midwinter solstices, or equinoxes. Due to precession (above right), this is 20.4 minutes shorter than* The Sidereal Year, *which is the length of time it takes the earth to orbit the sun in space. The constellation behind the spring equinox sun denotes the Great Month.*

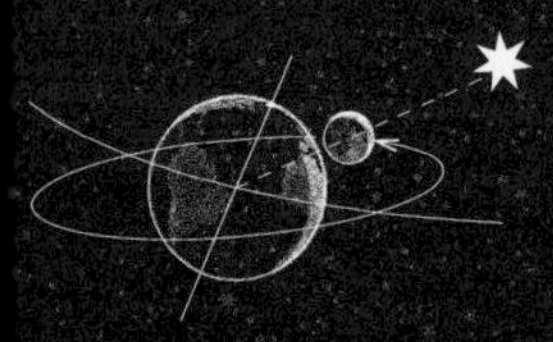

Sidereal Lunar Month

27.321661 days. *The length of time it takes the moon to return to a given star in the sky.*

Lunation

29.530588 days. *Also known as the* Synodic Lunar Month, *the length of time between new moons.*

Rotation of Moon's Nodes

18.612816 years. *The length of time it takes the moon's orbit to complete one wobble.*

The Earliest Calendars

scratches and scrapings on bone and stone

The earliest known calendars are all lunar. Simple midsummer or midwinter alignments probably sufficed to define the solar year, but when humans first started counting actual days, they seem to have counted them in relation to the moon.

In the 35,000 BC palaeolithic Lebombo bone (*lower, below*), from Swaziland, Africa, 29 clearly defined notches are carved into the fibula of a baboon, a useful record of the number of days between full moons. The 30,000 BC Blanchard Bone, discovered in Abri, France (*upper, below*) may, amongst other things, show the sequence of moon phase changes over two months, the more accurate formula of 59 days = 2 lunar cycles.

By neolithic times, as clearly evidenced both at the 3200 BC Irish site of Newgrange, and at 2500 BC Stonehenge in England, the Metonic cycle of 19 solar years = 235 lunations had been discovered. Stonehenge also displays the value of 29.5 days between moons as 29-and-a-half stones in its outer circle (the half-stone is still visible today, *opposite below*).

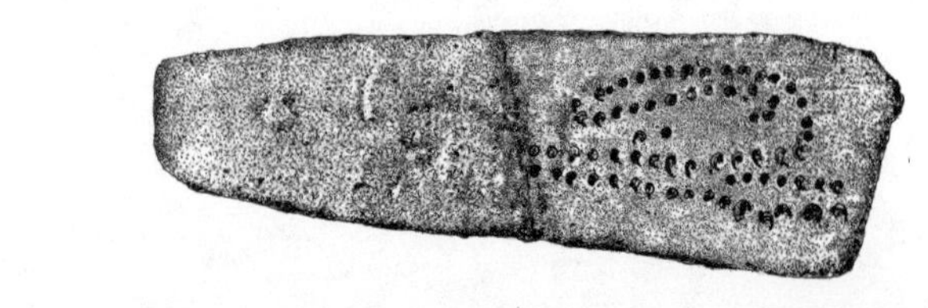

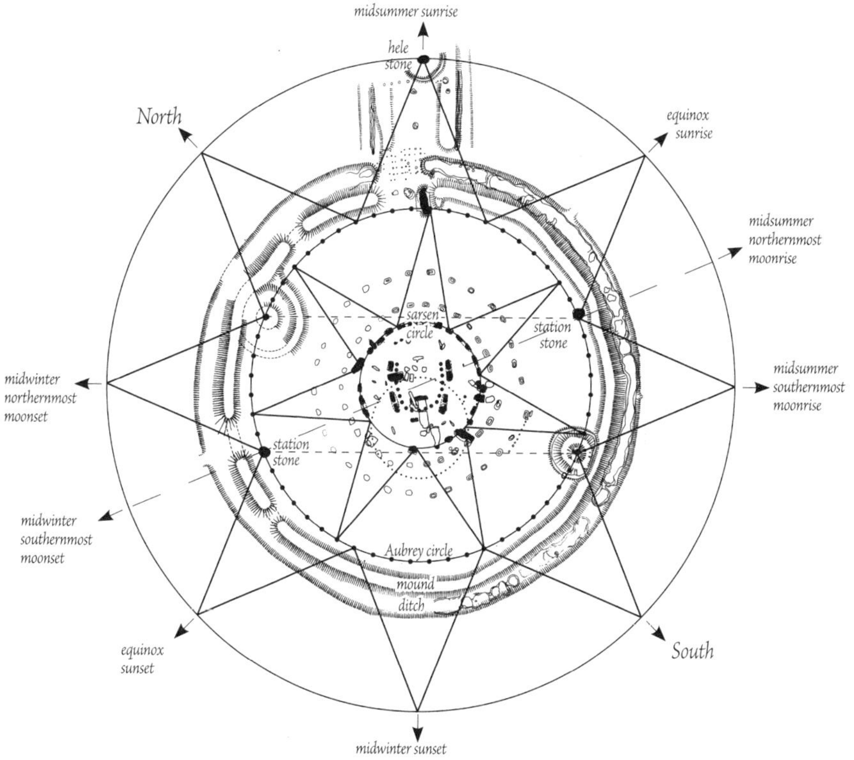

midsummer sunrise
hele stone
North
equinox sunrise
midsummer northernmost moonrise
sarsen circle
station stone
midwinter northernmost moonset
midsummer southernmost moonrise
station stone
midwinter southernmost moonset
Aubrey circle
mound
ditch
equinox sunset
South
midwinter sunset

Stonehenge displays the calendrical understanding of neolithic times. An outer 8-fold distribution of the sun and moon surrounds 56 Aubrey holes, used for eclipse prediction. These, by 7-fold geometry, enclose Stonehenge proper (below), with its 29.5 outer sarsen stones and 19 smaller inner bluestones.

Ancient China
an early system

The Chinese calendar was reputedly invented in 2637 BC by Emperor Huang Ti, and possibly replaced a 13-month, 384-day lunar calendar. In the Shang Dynasty (1800–1200 BC), the 19-year Metonic cycle of *intercalation* was used, a thousand years before Meton recorded it, as well as the related 76-year *Callipic* cycle (76 solar years = 940 lunations less a day).

In antiquity, the Chinese year started on the new moon nearest winter solstice, but in the late 2nd century BC, a calendar reform requiring winter solstice to occur in month 11 ushered in a new system of intercalation. The Chinese New Year now starts on the second new moon after winter solstice, with the seasons beginning at the cross-quarter midpoints between solstices and equinoxes.

The Chinese year consists of twelve months, each starting at midnight just before a new moon, and alternating between 29 and 30 days. To keep track with the solar year, every second or third year an extra *leap* month is added, called "the thirteenth month" (*see appendix p.52*). The years used to be counted from the accession of an emperor, but this was abolished after the 1911 revolution.

Each year is named after one of 12 zodiacal animals (*Rat; Ox; Tiger; Rabbit; Dragon; Snake; Horse; Sheep; Monkey; Rooster; Dog; Pig, below*), and one of the Chinese elements (*Wood, Fire, Earth, Metal and Water*), each element lasting two years (destructive then constructive), creating a 60-year cycle. The year 2000 (started late-February) was metal dragon, 2001 was metal snake, and 2002 was water horse, etc.

A decorated bronze mirror of the Tang Dynasty. The central circle shows a dragon, a phoenix, a tiger and a tortoise-snake representing the four quarters of the heavens (east, south, west, and north respectively). The next circle shows the twelve zodiacal animals. The rat is in the north, and the sequence runs clockwise. Surrounding this are the eight trigrams of the I Ching that generate the 64 hexagrams shown below. Next are the 28 "mini-constellations" marking the 28 mansions of the Moon. The last ring inside the border is a poem.

The I Ching, or Book of Changes, was devised by the Fu Hsi, a mythical sovereign of ancient China around 2800 BC. The I Ching consists of 64 hexagrams, each made of 6 lines that are either broken (yin) or unbroken (yang). The famous sequence shown here was devised by King Wen of Zhou around 1050 BC. The second hexagram of each pair is either an inversion or the opposite of the previous one. The 384 lines of the hexagrams almost certainly represent the 384 days of 13 full moons (a 13-lunar-month calendar first spotted by Terence McKenna).

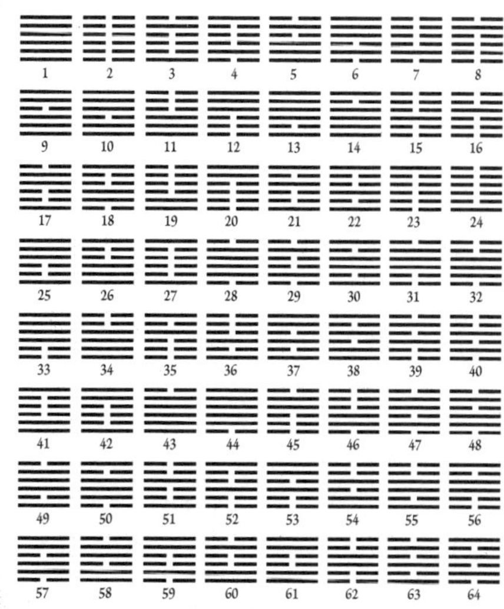

Ancient India
some seriously large numbers

There are varying accounts of the ancient Indian calendars. One mentioned in the 1st millennium BC *Mahâbhârata* mentions a year of "twelve months of 30 days, with a thirteenth month added every five years." This produces an average 366-day year (scholars have suggested a more accurate leap month would have been 26 or 27 days).

Lunar months began on the day after full moons in the north of India, but on the day after new moons in the south. From about 550 AD a luni-solar calendar was developed, with the lunar calendar fixed to a solar period, but, interestingly, it seems this may have been a sidereal year rather than a tropical one. This lasted until 1957, when it was replaced by the Gregorian calendar.

The *Vedas* (c.1500 BC) describe a series of very long cycles, some of which last trillions of years. At the shorter end of the spectrum we have the four Yugas: The *Krita* or *Satya Yuga* (Golden Age), lasting 1,728,000 years; the *Treta Yuga* (Silver Age), of 1,296,000 years; the *Dvapara Yuga* (Bronze Age), lasting 864,000 years, and the *Kali Yuga* (Iron Age), of 432,000 years. Some say we are currently leaving this dark Kali Yuga, the Iron Age of materialism, but Arab historian al-Bîrûnî (973-1048) said it only started around 3102 BC.

The Vedic numbers are all multiples of 2160 years, the traditional value for the time it takes the equinoctial Sun to precess through one sign of the zodiac. If we divide the ancient values by 360, the results echo another, older, Vedic version of events, where the Yugas are said to add to 24,000 years, a possible precessional value.

In Sri Yukteswar's early 20th century analysis (*opposite*), this reduced precessional scheme can be clearly seen.

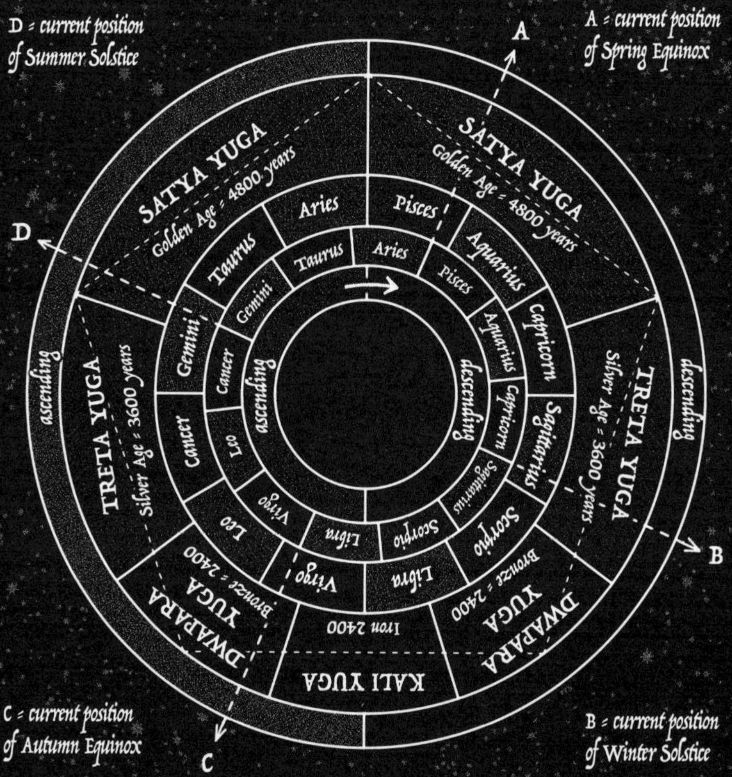

The Complete Yugic Calendar: Based on Sri Yukteswar's diagram, our slow passage through the Yugas takes a symmetrical form, with ascending and descending aspects. The two zodiacs are the sidereal (star-based, outer) and tropical (season-based, inner), which currently differ by nearly a whole sign. The spring (vernal) equinox denotes the current month in the precessional Great Year, while the autumn equinox produces the current Yuga. In other versions researchers have adjusted this diagram for the current precessional values.

SUMER AND BABYLON

the Muslim and Jewish lunar calendar

The Sumerian civilization started around 4000 BC and used a lunar year of 12 lunations (354 days). Months began with the observation at sunset of the new moon's first visible crescent and the years were recorded under the year number of the reigning king. The agricultural New Year was set after the autumn harvest.

By 3000 BC the Sumerians had adjusted their calendar to fit the sun, with twelve 30-day months, giving a 360-day year (between the solar and lunar years). The day was divided into twelve sections (equivalent to two hours), each subdivided into 30 parts (equal to four minutes). There were just two *seasons*—dry and wet.

By the time of ancient Babylon in 2000 BC, the twelve signs of the zodiac had been conceived. A lunar calendar again began to prevail, with the New Year starting at the first new moon after the spring equinox. A year of twelve lunar months was used, each alternating between 29 and 30 days, averaging close to the 29.53-day length of a lunation. Soon, a haphazard intercalation system evolved to keep the year in time with the seasons—each Sumerian city inserted extra months (three extra months over eight years), whenever they thought it appropriate. The practice was later centralized, with the king announcing the intercalary months, but by 500 BC the Babylonians were already using a system in which they had twelve years of twelve months each, and seven years of 13 months each, adding to a total of 235 months (the Metonic cycle again!).

From 1000 BC, the Babylonians recorded the *heliacal* ("with the Sun") *risings* and settings of certain stars. This star calendar consisted of a 360-day year made up of 12 months of 30 days each.

Sumer & Babylon: The calendar changed from a 354-day lunar year, to a 360-day luni-solar, to a Metonic system with intercalated months.

Ancient Egypt: The priests watched for the heliacal rise of Sirius (close to Orion/Osiris) coinciding with the Nile flood, to indicate the New Year.

Israel: The Jewish calendar is luni-solar - 12 lunar months with an intercalated 13th in some years, ensuring that Passover remained in Spring.

Baghdad: The Islamic calendar is lunar, and ignores the Sun. A year has 354 or 355 days, adding the extra day 11 times over 30 years, to keep up with the Moon.

ANCIENT EGYPT

heliacal risings and ancient zodiacs

The earliest calendar in Egypt dates to 5000 BC and was lunar, the months beginning as the old Moon disappeared just before dawn. Contrary to the Sumerian system, days thus began at sunrise, rather than sunset. The solar year was tracked by *Nilometers*, which measured the high water mark of the Nile, an annual recurrence.

By 2500 BC the lunar calendar had been adjusted to fit the year, which was now set by the more accurate annual heliacal rising of the bright Dog Star, Sirius, just a few days before the flooding of the Nile. The result was a year of twelve 30-day months, with five *epagomenal* days "added on" the end, giving a 365-day year.

However, without a leap-day, the year drifted through the seasons, slipping back a day every four years, taking 1461 *vague* years (of 365 days) before New Year again realigned with the rising of Sirius (so 1461 Egyptian or vague years = 1460 Julian years). This period is known as the *Sothic* cycle, after Sothis, or Sirius.

The Egyptians later adopted the Babylonian zodiac via the Greeks, and adapted the 36 *decans* as 10° each. Two examples of Egyptian zodiacs from Denderah are shown (*below and opposite*).

Opposite and above: Zodiacs from the Temple of Hathor, Denderah, dating to 30 BC. In the zodiac above the central figures represent the northern constellations surrounded by the twelve signs of the zodiac. The small figures holding staffs represent the planets, and surrounding these, on the edge of the central disc are the 36 decans (shown standing in boats opposite). The axis of the Temple, vertical in the zodiac above, was aligned to the heliacal rising of Sirius.

Metallic Memories

wizard's hats and early gearings

Little is known of early European calendars, but in 1999, a 12-inch "sky" Disc (dated to 1600 BC) was found at Nebra, near Goseck, Germany. It shows a sun and crescent moon close to the constellation of the Pleiades, the same pattern used by the Babylonians, 1,000 years later, to determine the time to intercalate a 13th month into their lunar calendar, harmonizing the lunar and solar years.

Four Bronze Age golden pointed "wizard's" hats, found in Switzerland, Germany and France (dated to 1300 BC) offer further clues. They are covered with sun and moon symbols, 1735 on one hat (1737 and 1739 on two of the others), which form a code corresponding almost exactly to the Metonic cycle.

In ancient Greece a calendar of 12 months was used, with a periodic 13th intercalated. As in Egypt, New Year coincided with the rising of Sirius. Meton recorded the 19-year cycle in 432 BC, but it had little effect on the calendar. In 1900 the remains of an extraordinary ancient Greek astronomical computer with 37 bronze gears was found in a shipwreck near the island of Antikythera. Dated to 150 BC, the front dial once displayed the solar cycle and zodiac, with sun, moon and lunar phase indicators; on the back two pointers showed the *Saros* and Callipic cycles. It could predict eclipses, and may have also tracked the positions of the planets.

The Coligny Calendar was engraved by druids on a bronze tablet around 180 AD, in the Gaulish language. A lunar year is recorded as twelve 29- or 30-day months with an extra month inserted every two and a half years, totaling 62 months over five years. Over 30 years, five of these 62-month cycles, plus one 61-month cycle were used.

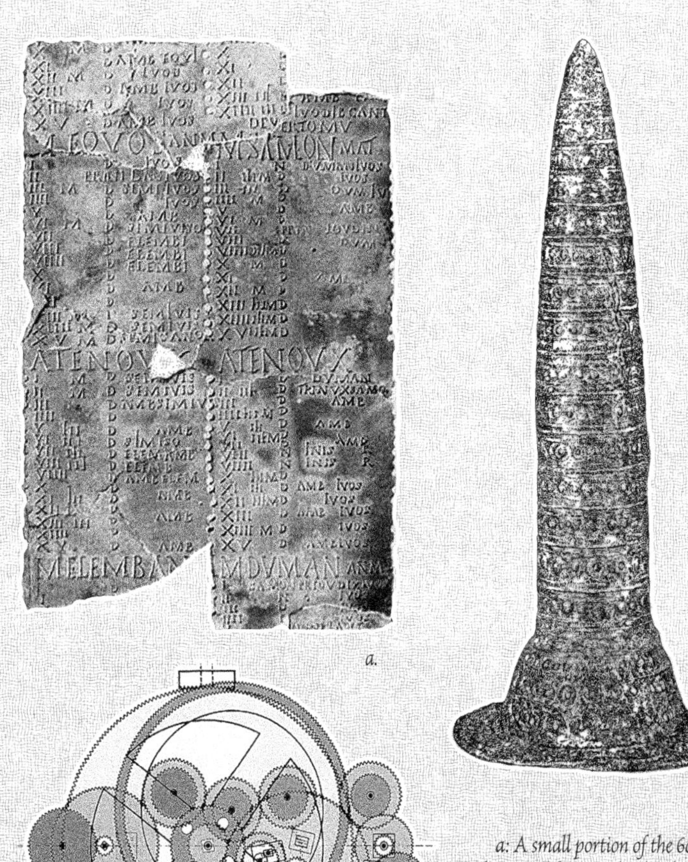

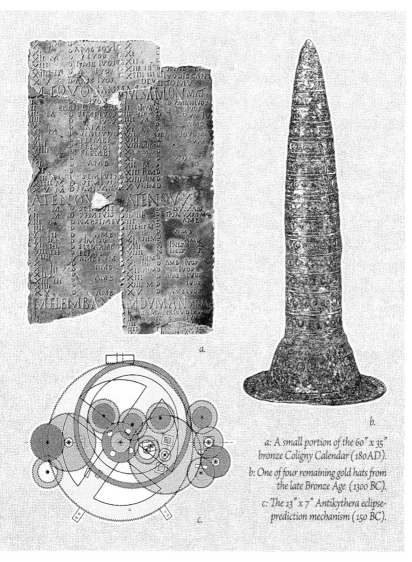

a: A small portion of the 60" x 35" bronze Coligny Calendar (180AD).

b: One of four remaining gold hats from the late Bronze Age (1300 BC).

c: The 13" x 7" Antikythera eclipse-prediction mechanism (150 BC).

The Roman Calendar
and great months and years

Throughout ancient Europe a secret longer cycle lay behind all other calendars, caused by the slow precession of the equinoxes (the *Great Year*). Every 2160 years (a *Great Month*) a new, younger, zodiacal sign appeared behind the equinoctial sun, heralding three 720-year decans with opposing rulerships (*see opposite top*).

The earliest Roman calendar replaced a lunar one. With ten (non-lunar) months of 30 or 31 days, it lasted 304 days, and September to December retain their positional names today. There was also a 61-day winter period outside the calendar. A reform in 713 BC changed the months to 29 days, adding a 29-day January and a 28-day February, resulting in a 355-day year. Every other year, a 27-day intercalary month was added at the end of February (which was shortened to 23 or 24 days). The two years, of 377 or 378 days, and 355 days, combined to give an average year of 366 or 366.5 days.

Finally, in 46 BC the *Julian calendar* was born, with Caesar instituting the 365-day, 12-month year that is familiar to us today, with one simple leap-day added to February every 4 years. However, the Julian calendar falls behind the solar year by 11 minutes per year, and by the 16th century, the discrepancy had added to 10 days. Accordingly, on 4th October 1582 the Julian Calendar was ended, 10 days deleted, and the following day, 15th October, became the first of the new *Gregorian calendar.* From now on, leap years were those divisible by 4, excluding those divisible by 100, but not by 400. The new year was 365.2425 days long, losing a day every 3,200 years.

With this new calendar, which we all use today, the moon was finally banished, the stars forgotten, and the sun ruled supreme.

AGE OF	DECAN	RULERSHIP	SYMBOL & EXAMPLE
TAURUS	1: 4320-3601 BC	Taurus (mature)	Bull Cults of Europe
	2: 3600-2881 BC	Scorpio at heart	Cults of the Dead
	3: 2880-2161 BC	Taurus (youthful)	The Sacrificial Calf
ARIES	1: 2160-1441 BC	Aries (mature)	The Ram, Moses
	2: 1440-721 BC	Libra at heart	Balance, Law
	3: 720-1 BC	Aries (youthful)	The Sacrificial Lamb
PISCES	1: 1-720 AD	Pisces (mature)	The Fish, Christ
	2: 721-1440 AD	Virgo at heart	Purity, Intellect, Islam
	3: 1441-2160 AD	Pisces (youthful)	Death of Small Fishes
AQUARIUS	1: 2161-3600 AD	Aquarius (mature)	Community and Water
	2: 3601-4320 AD	Leo at heart	Return of the King
	3: 4321-5040 AD	Aquarius (young)	etc etc etc

Above: A portion of the western classical Great Year, showing the divisions into decans and their rulerships.

A K·IAN·F	H K·FEB·N	D K·MAR·NP	C K·APR·F	A K·MAI·F	H K·IVN·N	F K·IVL·N	E K·AVG·F	D K·SEP·F	B K·OCT·N	A K·NOV·F	G K·DEC·N
B F	A N	E F	D F	B F	A F	G N	F F	E F	C F	B F	H N
C C	B N	F C	E C	C C	B C	H N	G C	F C	D C	C C	A N
D C	C N	G C	F C	D C	C C	A N	H C	G C	E C	D C	B C
E NON·F	D NON·N	H C	G NON·N	E C	D NON·N	B POPLI·NP	A NON·F	H NON·F	F C	E NON·F	C NON·F
F F	E N	A C	H N	F C	E N	C N	B F	A F	G C	F F	D F
G C	F N	B NON·F	A N	G NON·F	F N	D NON·N	C C	B C	H NON·F	G C	E C
H C	G N	C F	B N	H F	G N	E N	D C	C C	A F	H C	F C
A AGON·NP	H N	D C	C N	A LEM·N	H VEST·N	F N	E C	D C	B C	A C	G C
B C	A N	E C	D N	B C	A N	G C	F C	E C	C C	B C	H C
C CAR·NP	B N	F C	E N	C LEM·N	B MATR·N	H C	G C	F C	D MEDI·NP	C C	A AGON·NP
D C	C N	G C	F N	D C	C N	A C	H C	G C F	E C	D C	B EN
E IDVS·NP	D IDVS·NP	H EN	G IDVS·NP	E LEM·NP	D IDVS·NP	B C	A IDVS·NP	H IDVS·NP	F FONT·NP	E IDVS·NP	C IDVS·NP
F EN	E N	A EQVIR·NP	H N	F C	E N	C C	B F	A F	G EN	F F	D F
G CAR·NP	F LVPER·NP	B IDVS·NP	A FORDI·NP	G IDVS·N	F Q·ST·D F	D IDVS·NP	C C	B C F	H IDVS·NP	G C	E CONS·NP
H C	G EN	C F	B N	H F	G C	E C	D C	C C	A F	H C	F C
A C	H QVIR·NP	D LIBER·NP	C N	A C	H C	F F	E PORT·NP	D C	B C	A C	G SATVR·NP
B C	A C	E C	D N	B C	A C	G C	F C	E C	C C	B C	H C
C C	B C	F QVIN·NP	E CERIA·NP	C C	B C	H LVCAR·NP	G VINAL·	F C	D ARMI·NP	C C	A OPA·NP
D C	C C	G C	F N	D C	C C	A C	H C	G C	E C	D C	B C
E C	D FERA·F	H C	G PARIL·NP	E AGON·NP	D C	B LVCAR·NP	A CONS·NP	H C	F C	E C	C DIVAL·NP
F C	E C	A N F	H N	F N F	E C	C C	B EN	A C	G C	F C	D C
G C	F TERM·NP	B TVBIL·NP	A VINAL·F	G TVBIL·NP	F C	D NEPT·NP	C VOLK·NP	B C	H C	G C	E LARE·NP
H C	G REGIF·N	C Q·R·C·F F	B C	H Q·R·C·F F	G C	E C	D C	C C	A C	H C	F C
A C	H C	D C	C ROBIG·NP	A C	H C	F FVR·NP	E OPIC·NP	D C	B C	A C	G C
B C	A EN	E C	D C	B C	A C	G N	F C	E C	C C	B C	H C
C C	B EQVIR·NP	F C	E C	C C	B C	H C	G VOLT·NP	F C	D C	C C	A C
D C	C C	G C	F C	D C	C C	A C	H C	G C	E C	D C	B C
E C		H C	G C	E C	D C	B C	A C	H C	F C	E C	C C
F C		A C	H C	F C	E C	C C	B C	A C	G C	F C	D C
G C		B C		G C		D C	C C		H C		E C
XXXI	XXIIX	XXXI	XXX	XXXI	XXX	XXXI	XXXI	XXX	XXXI	XXX	XXXI

Above: A Roman Calendar. The days were assigned letters (A-H), with A being market days. Running down the columns: the first day of each month was known as the Kalends (K); the Nones (NON) were usually the 5th, 6th or 7th day; the Ides (IDVS) were in the middle, on the 13th, 14th or 15th. Other letters to the sides of the days meant: Dies fasti (F), legal proceedings and/or voting day; Dies nefasti (NP), no legal matters or voting today; additional special festivals (eg SATVR, the Saturnalia from 17-23 Dec).

Another World

a lost civilization

As we have seen, despite the best efforts of kings, priests and calendar-makers throughout the world, calendrical systems remained essentially imperfect efforts at reconciling the Sun and the Moon into everyday life. In fact, very little had really surprised classical scholars for some time until the 19th century, when reports of strange ruins began to appear from the Central American jungle. These rainforest temples were covered in obscure carvings which were to revolutionize the understanding of ancient timekeeping. It was not until the end of the 19th century that an Amercian newspaper editor, John Goodman, took the first steps in the advanced decoding of the extraordinary calendrical achievements of this lost world. The rest of this book examines what is now termed the *Mayan Calendar.*

We now know that the ancient Maya lived in the areas which today form south-east Mexico (parts of the Mexican states of Tabasco and Chiapas), the Yucatan peninsula, Guatemala, Belize, North-West Honduras and North-West El Salvador. Also clear is the fact that the entire region flowered in a great golden age, comparable to that of ancient Greece. In this *Classic* period, dating from 250 - 900 AD, large-scale construction and urbanization accompanied considerable intellectual and artistic development, including the perfection of the ancient calendar. Suddenly, around 900 AD, for reasons that are still debated, many of the cities in the southern Mayan area were abandoned. Subsequently, during the *Post-Classic* period (900 - 1521 AD) the Maya, Toltecs, Aztecs, and Itza-Maya used a reduced version of the calendar. The Spanish Conquistadors arrived in 1519, conquering the Aztecs, and in 1521 the descendants of the Classic Maya.

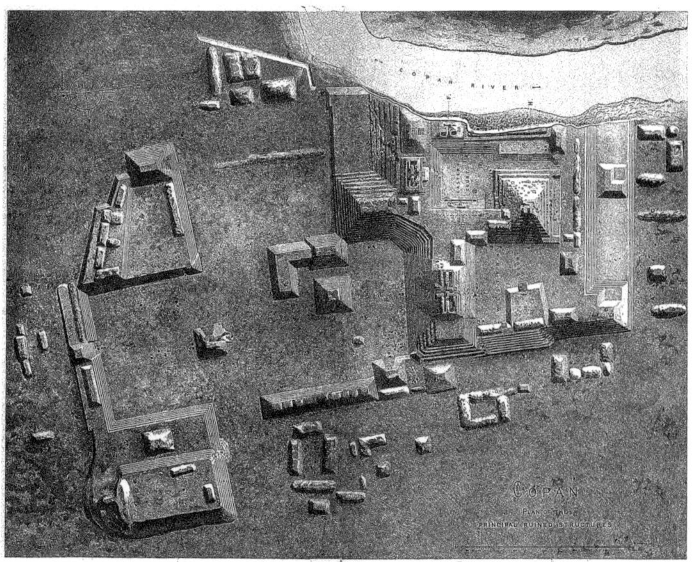
COPAN RIVER
COPAN
PLAN OF THOSE
PRINCIPAL RUINED STRUCTURES

Surviving Manuscripts

the vanity of Spanish bonfires

The Mesoamericans recorded information via stone inscriptions and books with painted glyphs and images. On arrival, the Spanish declared all local writings to be "works of the devil" and made huge bonfires of any books they found. Today, just fifty pre-Columbian manuscripts survive, and only four of these are Maya *codices*.

The surviving four codices (*shown opposite*) all date to the Post-Classic period, and are probably from the Yucatan peninsula. The *Dresden Codex* is the best preserved and most important of the four. Bought for Dresden library in 1739 from a private collector, it suffered some water damage in World War II when Dresden was bombed, but was recovered. Its 39 leaves are a treatise on divination and astronomy, with Sun, Moon, and Venus tables. Dated to the early 13th century, it is probably partially copied from earlier books.

The *Paris Codex* was rediscovered in the Paris library in 1859, and is in very poor condition—only the central glyphs and pictures on its 11 leaves have survived. It contains a katun sequence (a series of thirteen 20-year cycles), with associated deities and ceremonies and a partial depiction of a thirteen-sign Maya zodiac, with scorpion, turtle, rattlesnake, and bat all remaining visible.

The *Madrid Codex* was found in two parts in Spain in the 1860s, and consists of 56 leaves. Full of horoscopes and almanacs, it contains fewer astronomical tables than the Dresden Codex. The year-bearers are shifted forward one day from the ones shown in the other codices, indicating a possible origin in West Yucatan.

Discovered in Mexico in 1965, the 11-page bark-paper *Grolier Codex* is a simple Venus almanac. It may well be a clever forgery.

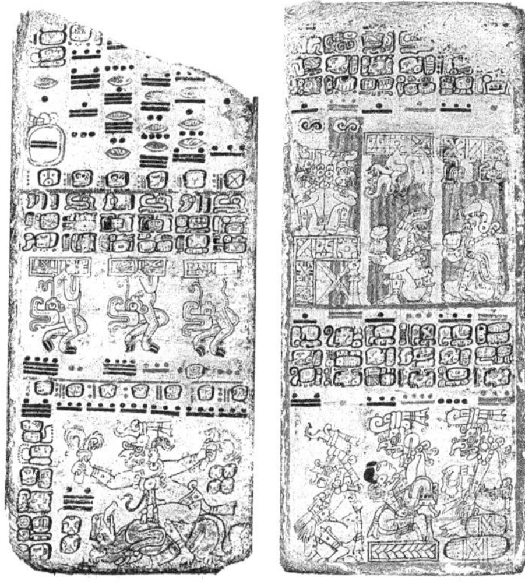

The Dresden Codex - with Mars beasts hanging from sky-bands

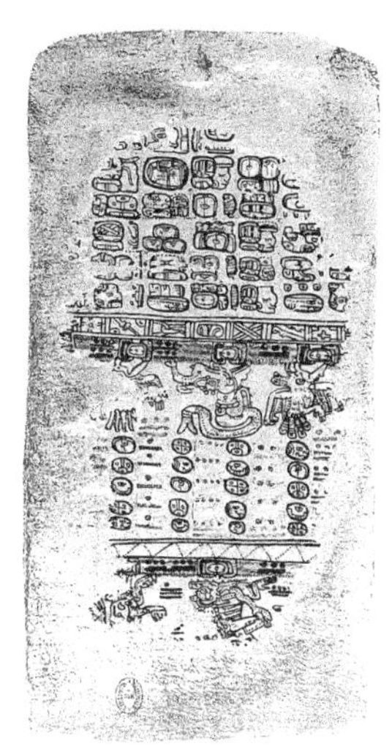

The Paris Codex - with zodiac signs

The Madrid Codex - an astronomer observes a star via a zenith tube

The Grolier Codex - a Venus table

THE NUMBERING SYSTEM

fingers and toes

The counting system we use today is called *place numeration*, in which there is a position for units, and further placed positions for multiples of those units. This ingenious technique is thought to have originated in India around the 8th century, passing via Arabia to Moorish Spain. However, we now know that place numeration and the concept of zero had already been in use in Mesoamerica for over a thousand years. Our decimal, or base-10 system, has units, 10's, 100's, 1000's, and so on; the Maya instead used a vigesimal, or base-20 system, with units, 20's, 400's, 8000's, etc.

In our decimal system, the positions increase by a factor of ten from right to left, and are read from left to right. In the Mayan system, the positions increase by a factor of twenty from bottom to top, and are read from top to bottom. There is an exception—when recording dates in the long count calendar, the third position represents only 18 times the second position, giving a 360-day unit instead of a 400-day one, and thus approximating the solar year.

The Maya used three types of notation for recording numbers. These were the bar-and-dot numerals (*opposite top*), the rarer head-variant numerals (*see caption opposite top*), and the very rare full-figure glyphs (*lower opposite*). Zero is represented by a shell glyph in the codices, and by half a quatrefoil flower (*below*) in the inscriptions. The full quatrefoil represents the 260-day calendar in the *Fejervary Codex* and the *Madrid Codex* (*see page 27*).

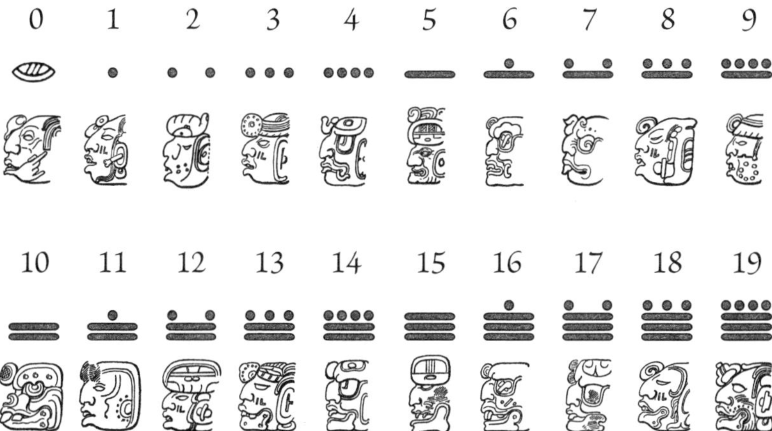

The dot-bar system probably originated using stone, twigs and seashells, with a stick representing the number 5. In the head-variants a different human head represents zero to twelve, except for ten, which is a death's head or skull. For the 'teens, thirteen to nineteen, the heads of numerals three to nine are used with an additional fleshless jawbone from the skull of number ten.

Full figure glyph numerals depict the heads with bodies attached. For example, zero uinals is a man with a forehead attachment and a hand-jaw (zero) shown wrestling with an amphibian (uinal).

Incredible Calendars

where did they come from?

The Maya used a bewildering number of different cycles in their calendar, the reasons for which will become clear later. In the reference table (*opposite*) these are given with their day-counts and algebraic relationships. As a day-count, the Maya system can compute many millions of days into the past or future, but is not linked to the seasons like the Gregorian calendar, since there is no intercalation. The Maya tracked various cycles, including the solar year, but uniquely, they didn't try to combine them into one calendar—they cross-referenced their calendars instead.

Scholars are still unsure as to the exact origins of this complex system, particularly the central Tzolkin-Haab device. The history of the ancestors of the Maya stretches back to the *Palaeo-Indian* period (20,000 - 8,000 BC) when Siberian hunter-gatherers colonized the New World, slowly settling during the *Archaic* period (8,000 - 2,000 BC), domesticating maize and building permanent settlements. In the *Pre-Classic* (Formative) period (2,000 BC - 250 AD) civilization began, with small towns and fertility cults.

Elements of the calendar may date back to the earliest civilizations of Mesoamerica (the so-called "Olmec"), as early as 1500 BC, or the Zapotec (600 BC onwards) before being perfected by the Maya themselves (200 BC onwards). The oldest Long Count date is from an Olmec site but Tzolkin dates from 600 BC and 650 BC have been found at Zapotec and (recently) Olmec sites respectively.

There is fascinating evidence that the Berber peoples of north-west Africa also used a cycle of 520 days (twice a Tzolkin) on the Atlantic islands of Tenerife and Grand Canary.

	Name	Length	Composition
Basic units			
a	Earth God Cycle	7 days	
b	Lords of the Night	9 days	
c	Heaven God Cycle	13 days	
d	Uinal	20 days	
e	Lunar cycle	29 alt 30 days	
f	Two moon cycle	59 days	2*e*
Years			
g	Tzolkin	260 days	*cd*
h	Tun	360 days	2*bd*
i	Computing Year	364 days	4*ac*
j	Haab	365 days	2*bd* + 5
Planet Cycles			
k	Venus cycle	584 days	73 x 8
l	Mars cycle	780 days	3 tzolkins (*g*)
m	Jupiter/Saturn cycle	819 days	*abc*
n	3 Eclipse Year cycle	1040 days	4 tzolkins (*g*)
Rounds			
p	Calendar Round	18,980 days	52 haabs (*j*), 73 tzolkins (*g*)
q	Venus Round	2 Calendar Rounds	65*k*, 104*j*, 146*g*
r	Mars Round	6 Calendar Rounds	146*l*, 195*k*, 312*j*, 438*g*
Long Count			
s	Katun	7,200 days	20 tun (*h*)
t	Baktun	144,000 days	20 katun (*s*), 400*h*
u	Sun	5,125 years	13 baktun (*t*), 260*s*, 5200*h*
v	Precessional	25,626 years	5 suns (*u*), 26000*h*, 36000*g*

The Tzolkin

260 days

The Tzolkin is a sacred 260-day almanac that determined the ceremonies and prophecies of the Maya. Each day the day-numbers and day-sign progressed by one, so that 1 Imix was followed by 2 Ik, 3 Akbal, and so on (*see diagram opposite*). The two qualities influencing any particular day in the cycle of 260 were believed to determine the character traits and destiny of anyone born on that day, and they were often named after the combination. The 13-day period within which a person was born is today called a *trecena.*

This 13 x 20 day-count has been in daily use by the Quiche calendar priests, or daykeepers of the Guatemala highlands, in an unbroken chain since Classic times. The Quiche call it the *ch'olk'ij*, "count of days" ("Tzolkin" in Yucatec). The Mexica, or Aztecs of central Mexico, also followed the 260-day count, calling it the *tonalpohualli*, with similar signs on the same days as the Maya.

The Quiche Maya say the Tzolkin is actually based on the period of human gestation and the maize agricultural cycle. The system was also used as an *augury*, the daykeeper being consulted to divine whether or not a day was suitable for performing various activities.

Scholars believe the day was once counted from sunrise, but the present-day Jacalteca and Ixil Maya groups both count from sunset.

THE TZOLKIN

13 NUMBERS COMBINE WITH 20 DAY-SIGNS

Each day-sign and each number is associated with a particular god, so that every one of the 260 days consists of a unique combination of two influences, or "energetic qualities."

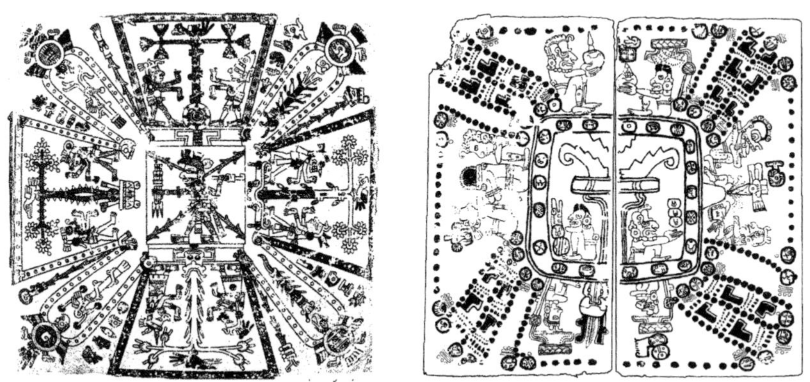

Two Tzolkins, from the Fejervary Codex (left) and Madrid Codex (right), each with 260 small dots in their outlines. The 260 days may have referred to the period of human gestation.

THE HAAB

(18 x 20) +5 = 365 days

The *vague* year or Haab (*xiuhpohualli* to the Aztecs), consisted of eighteen months of twenty days each (*shown below*), plus a nineteenth month of five unlucky days, known as Uayeb, (*nemontemi* to the Aztecs). The Haab thus totaled 365 days (no leap days were added).

Each month ran from 0–19, with the first day termed a *seating* day. For the Maya, the signature of time cycles could be detected in advance, so the last day of each month was the seating of the next.

The Maya New Years Day was on 1 Pop and the *year-bearer* was the day in the Tzolkin that corresponded to this in the Haab, and gave its name (and influence) to the Haab that followed. Only four of the day-signs coincide with 1 Pop and in Classic times these were Akbal, Lamat, Ben and Etznab. Given the 13 number variations of each sign, there were thus 4 x 13, or 52 possible year-bearers. In fact, there are five theoretically possible year-bearer groups, (since 4 x 5 = 20: the number of day-signs), but only four are known to have been in use. For example, the year-bearers shifted forward one position in Post-Classic times (to Kan, Muluc, Ix and Cauac) in the Yucatan peninsula, for unknown reasons.

Some groups (including the Aztecs), used a terminal year-bearer system, in which the year is named after the 360th day.

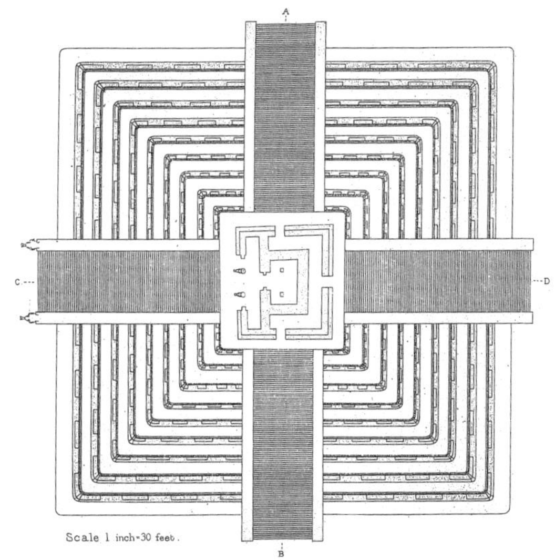

Left: The Pyramid of Kukulcan, also known as El Castillo, at Chichen Itza in the Yucatan. Each side has 91 steps, which sum to 364, the number of days in the Computing Year. 91 is 7 x 13 and the sum of 1-13. The top platform represents the 365th step.

Below: The Pyramid of the Niches at El Tajin near Papantla in Veracruz, Mexico, has only one stairway, on the east side, and a total of 365 niches. There was originally a temple on the summit, now crumbled away.

The Calendar Round
52 years

The same combination of day positions in the Tzolkin and Haab calendars does not recur until 52 haabs, or 73 tzolkins have passed, a total of 18,980 days (*see opposite top*). The Maya name for this 52-year period is lost, though the Aztecs called it *xiuhmolpilli* "year fire bundle" (*below*), and Mayanists today term it the *Calendar Round*.

Little is known of the Mayan customs around the Calendar Round, but the Aztec traditions are well preserved. They expected the world to end at the close of a Calendar Round, and every 52 years, on the last night, the inhabitants of Tenochtitlan (where Mexico City now stands), extinguished all their fires, swept their houses, threw their statues into water and gathered at an extinct volcano known as the Hill of the Star. The priests climbed the hill at sunset to observe the stars. A captive warrior was sacrificed and his heart torn out. A new fire was kindled in his chest cavity and torches were taken from this to re-light all the temple fires and from these, the hearths in all the homes. Much feasting followed.

The event is known as the *New Fire* ceremony and scholars now think it started with the people who built Teotihuacan, later being passed on via the Toltecs to the Aztecs. The Maya were also practicing the ceremony in late Classic times at Chichen Itza.

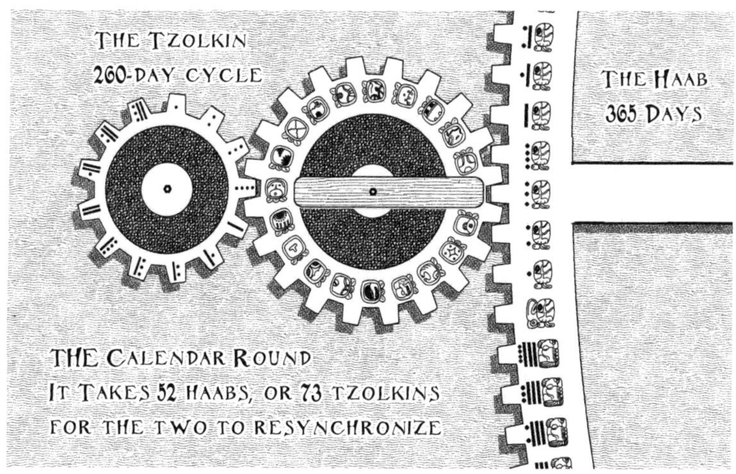

Above: After 52 haabs, when the Tzolkin and Haab positions once again reach the same combination as when you were born, the Maya and other Mesoamerican cultures considered you become an elder. In the Gregorian calendar this is 13 days before your 52nd birthday (since the haabs exclude leap days). Below: The Aztec city of Tenochtitlan, site of Mexico City. Buildings were relayered every 52 years.

VENUS IN THE CALENDAR

it all makes sense

Venus was known to the Maya as *Noh ek* or *Xux ek* - the "great star" or "wasp star" respectively, and it is in the light of the motions of Earth's closest planetary neighbor that the unadjusted Haab really makes sense as a calendrical unit. The bright sparkling point of light that is Venus disappears into the glare of the sun for about two weeks as it passes in front, before rising as the morning star, disappearing again for 13 weeks behind the sun, and then reappearing as the evening star. This is the *synodic* cycle of Venus, and it repeats five times over eight years (*see opposite*). The average time between synods (conjunctions with the sun) is 583.92 days, which the Maya rounded off to 584 (there was a system by which to correct the accumulated error). The Mayan glyph for Venus was a wriggly line with "eyes" or, sometimes, a four-pointed star (*below*).

Five synodic cycles of Venus repeat after 2920 days (584 x 5), exactly eight haabs (8 x 365=2920), almost exactly 13 Venus years (13 x 224.7 = 2921.1 days), and very close to 99 lunations.

After two Calendar Rounds (104 haabs or 146 tzolkins), exactly 65 Venus cycles, or 13 Venus pentagrams will have occurred (*see opposite*). This period is therefore known as the *Venus Round* (*Huehuetiliztli* to the Aztecs), and small adjustments were made at this time.

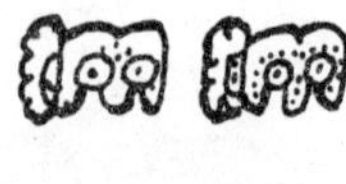

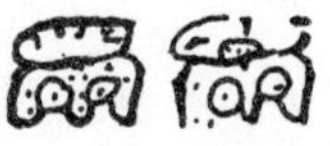

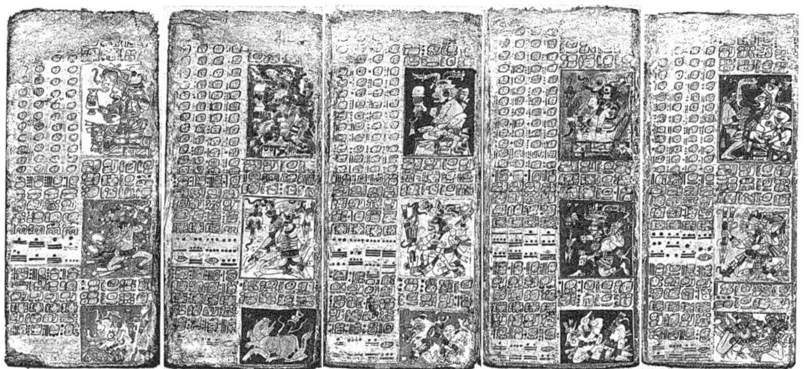

The five Venus panels from the Dresden Codex, recording three 104-haab Venus rounds. In the first the count is adjusted back 8 days at the end of the 57th Venus cycle, and a further 4 days back at the end of the 61st Venus cycle of the 2nd Venus round. The rounds thus overlap, and synchronize the rise of the morning star with the Tzolkin day 1 Ahau, as closely as possible. Accurate to .08 days in 468 years.

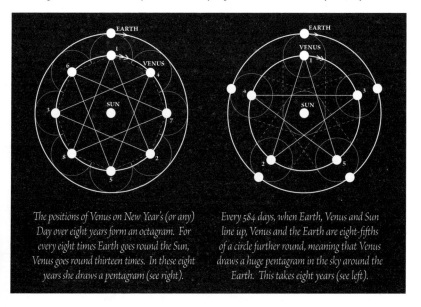

The positions of Venus on New Year's (or any) Day over eight years form an octagram. For every eight times Earth goes round the Sun, Venus goes round thirteen times. In these eight years she draws a pentagram (see right).

Every 584 days, when Earth, Venus and Sun line up, Venus and the Earth are eight-fifths of a circle further round, meaning that Venus draws a huge pentagram in the sky around the Earth. This takes eight years (see left).

The Moon
and Lords of the Night

The lunar month (lunation) is 29.53059 days in length. In the *Dresden Codex*, the eclipse table (*opposite*) consists of 405 lunations, equating to exactly 46 tzolkins. This and other extremely accurate Mayan formulations are shown in the table (*lower opposite*).

The *Dresden Codex* shows how the lunar months were arranged, with alternating lunations of 29 days and 30 days, plus interpolated extra 30-day months to keep the discrepancy below one day at all times. The Codex records 405 consecutive lunar months in 60 groups of six lunations each, plus nine interpolated groups of five lunations each. Fifty-four groups of the 60 consist of three 29-day months and three 30-day months (54 x 177 days), the other six consisting of two 29-day months and four 30-day months (6 x 178 days). The nine groups of five lunations consist of two 29-day months and three 30-day months (9 x 148 days). In all this totals 11,958 days, two days less than 46 tzolkins (11,960 days).

Since 3 *eclipse years* (of 346.62 days) are almost exactly equal to 4 tzolkins, eclipse prediction was especially simple for the Maya.

A series of nine Gods of the Lower World (Night Lords, Lords of the Underworld), the *Bolontiku*, ruled each day in turn (*below*). On stelae, the Night Lord is usually depicted after the long count and Tzolkin date, before the lunar glyphs and Haab date. The beginning/end day of every *tun* coincides with Night Lord Nine, since 360 = 9 x 40.

First

Second

Third

Fourth

Fifth

Sixth

Seventh

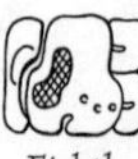
Eighth

Ninth

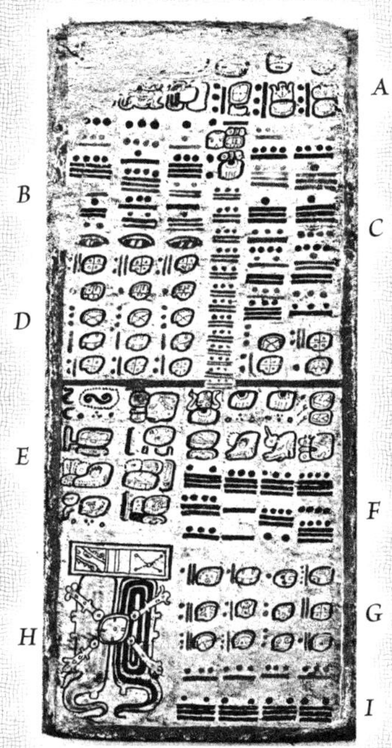

Left: The first of eight pages of lunar and eclipse tables from the Dresden Codex. Area A: Augury & omen glyphs. B: Multiples of table length. C: Long Count dates. D: Table entry points (lubs). E: Augury & omen glyphs. F: Cumulatives. G: Tzolkin dates. H: Eclipse picture. I: 177- & 148-day intervals.

Each group of lunations is followed by an interval or eclipse window when a solar eclipse would be visible somewhere on earth, so the table was probably used for predicting solar and lunar eclipses. Despite being dated to 755 AD, it could have been used to accurately predict eclipses beyond the 14th century. The 11,958 days were adjusted to 11,959 and 11,960 days so that a lub, or recurring Tzolkin base date, could be used as in the Venus calendar. In the case of the Eclipse table, the base date was 12 Lamat.

Below: Various moon glyphs.

PREDICTING FULL MOONS

Palenque: 81 moons = 2392 days.

2392 = 8 x 13 x 23 and 81 = 3 x 3 x 3 x3 [acc to 30 mins over the 6.5 years]

Copan: 149 moons = 4,400 days

4,400 = 11 x 20 x 20 [acc to 83 mins over the 12 years]

Dresden Codex: 405 moons = 11,960 days.

46 tzolkins. 405 = 5 x 81 (as Palenque above) [acc to 160 mins over the 33 years]

PREDICTING ECLIPSES

3 Eclipse Years = 4 tzolkins [acc to 3 hours over the 2.8 year cycle]

MARS, JUPITER AND SATURN

the mysterious 819-day cycle

Mars has a synodic cycle of 780 days, multiples of which are recorded in the Dresden Codex. This, importantly, is equivalent to three tzolkins. The Codex also shows 78-day periods of *retrograde* movement of Mars, with "Mars Beasts" suspended from sky bands (*see page 21*) when this occured while crossing the Milky Way.

After six Calendar Rounds (three Venus Rounds), the Mars cycle again comes into synchronization with the Tzolkin and Haab. This is the *Mars Round*. 146 Mars cycles = 312 haabs = 438 tzolkins.

The earth itself had seven layers, and seven corresponding gods, possibly called *Ah Uuc-Cheknal*. The Thirteen Gods of the Upper World, the Nine Lords of the Underworld, and the Seven Earth Gods together ruled a period called the 819-day cycle (7 x 9 x 13 = 819), the coincidence of their three periods. 819 is also 9 x 91.

The 819-day cycle is thought to have originated in Palenque. It has a common factor of 21 (21 x 13 x 3) with the synodic cycles of both Jupiter (21 x 19 days) and Saturn (21 x 18 days), whose movements were tracked by the Classic Maya, and recorded in the inscriptions on occasions when the current katun-ending coincided with a solar or lunar relationship, or both.

Each 819-day cycle is associated with a direction and color, a set of four (red/east, yellow/south, black/west, white/north), making a larger 3276-day cycle. In less than 16 years, the Tzolkin aligns the synodic periods of the Moon and all visible planets to within 4.31 days. It is the perfect interlock cycle: 42 tropical years = 59 tzolkins; 405 lunar months = 46 tzolkins; 61 Venus cycles = 137 tzolkins; One Mars cycle = three tzolkins; 88 Jupiter cycles = 135 tzolkins.

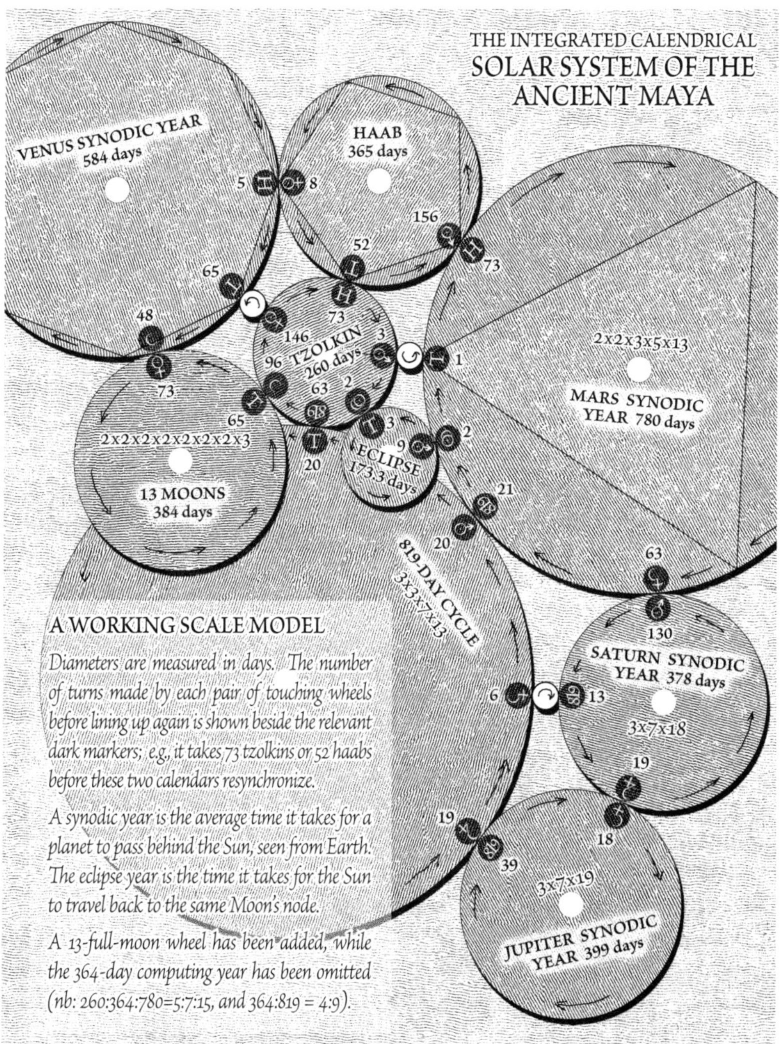
THE INTEGRATED CALENDRICAL
SOLAR SYSTEM OF THE
ANCIENT MAYA
VENUS SYNODIC YEAR
584 days
HAAB
365 days
TZOLKIN
260 days
2x2x3x5x13
MARS SYNODIC
YEAR 780 days
2x2x2x2x2x2x2x3
13 MOONS
384 days
ECLIPSE
173.3 days
819-DAY CYCLE
3x3x7x13
SATURN SYNODIC
YEAR 378 days
3x7x18
3x7x19
JUPITER SYNODIC
YEAR 399 days
A WORKING SCALE MODEL
Diameters are measured in days. The number of turns made by each pair of touching wheels before lining up again is shown beside the relevant dark markers; e.g., it takes 73 tzolkins or 52 haabs before these two calendars resynchronize.
A synodic year is the average time it takes for a planet to pass behind the Sun, seen from Earth. The eclipse year is the time it takes for the Sun to travel back to the same Moon's node.
A 13-full-moon wheel has been added, while the 364-day computing year has been omitted (nb: 260:364:780=5:7:15, and 364:819 = 4:9).

THE LONG COUNT

measuring whole epochs

The Calendar Round could only pinpoint a day within a 52-year period. To record dates centuries in the future and past, a more comprehensive system was required. By the first century BC, the Long Count calendar had been developed for this purpose. As in our own calendar, which counts from the birth of Christ, the Long Count starts at a base date, the first day of the current creation. According to Maya mythology, the world has gone through a series of eras, and the current era started on the day of creation—August 11th 3114 BC, recorded as 13.0.0.0.0 4 Ahau 8 Cumku.

Although the date would have originally been read from top to bottom, Mayanists today write the dates from left to right to ease interpretation and printing. Many also refer to the Day of Creation in 3114 BC as 0.0.0.0.0 rather than 13.0.0.0.0, to distinguish between the creation day at the start of the current 13-baktun cycle and the next one, at the end of it.

When the count reaches 13 baktuns, which is a period of 1,872,000 days, 5,200 tuns, or just over 5,125 solar years, a new creation occurs. The current 13-baktun cycle will be completed on 21st December 2012 AD, which is the next Day of Creation (*for information on larger cycles, see appendix p.55*).

20 KINS = 1 UINAL = 20 DAYS
18 UINALS = 1 TUN = 360 DAYS
20 TUNS = 1 KATUN = 7,200 DAYS
20 KATUNS = 1 BAKTUN = 144,000 DAYS
13 BAKTUNS = 1 SUN = 1,872,000 DAYS

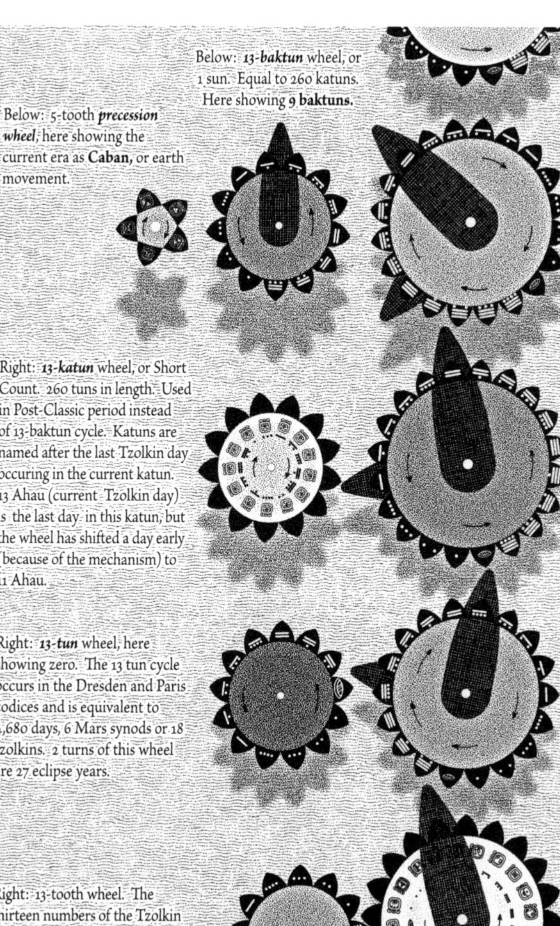

Below: **13-*baktun*** wheel, or 1 sun. Equal to 260 katuns. Here showing **9 baktuns.**

Left: Continuing vertically, 20-tooth ***pictun, calabtun, kinchiltun*** and ***alautun*** wheels.

Below: 5-tooth ***precession wheel***, here showing the current era as **Caban**, or earth movement.

Left: 20-tooth ***baktun*** wheel. 20 katuns are 1 baktun. The tooth last struck from the katun wheel (*below*) is 17, so the date is **17 katuns**. Each turn of this wheel advances the pictun wheel (*above*) and the 13-baktun wheel (*left*) by one baktun.

Right: **13-*katun*** wheel, or Short Count. 260 tuns in length. Used in Post-Classic period instead of 13-baktun cycle. Katuns are named after the last Tzolkin day occuring in the current katun. 13 Ahau (current Tzolkin day) is the last day in this katun, but the wheel has shifted a day early (because of the mechanism) to 11 Ahau.

Left: 20-tooth ***katun*** wheel. 20 tuns are 1 katun. The tooth last struck from the tun wheel (*below*) is zero, so the date is **zero tuns**. Each turn of this wheel advances the baktun wheel (*above*) and the 13-katun wheel (*left*) by one katun.

Right: **13-*tun*** wheel, here showing zero. The 13 tun cycle occurs in the Dresden and Paris codices and is equivalent to 4,680 days, 6 Mars synods or 18 tzolkins. 2 turns of this wheel are 27 eclipse years.

Left: 18-tooth ***tun*** wheel. 18 uinals are 1 tun. The tooth just struck from the uinal wheel (*below*) is zero, so the date is **zero uinals**. Each turn of the wheel advances the katun wheel (*above*) and the 13-tun wheel (*left*) by one tun.

Right: 13-tooth wheel. The thirteen numbers of the Tzolkin that combine with the 20 days-signs to give the Tzolkin date, in this case **13 Ahau**.

Left: 20-tooth ***uinal*** wheel. 20 kins (days) are 1 uinal. Each turn of the wheel advances the tun wheel (*above*) by one uinal. The inner ring is the Long Count kin number, here **zero kin**. This wheel is also the day-sign wheel of the Tzolkin (here Ahau as shown in the outer ring).

Stray's Olde MAYAN LONG COUNT MECHANISM patent pending

The Stelae

carved in stone

Stelae are inscribed stone pillars, erected to commemorate events. At the top of a typical stela an introductory glyph announces the following glyphs as a Long Count date. A variable element at the center of the introductory glyph is usually the glyph of the deity who is patron of the relevant "month" of the Haab.

Under the introductory glyph can be found up to 20 rows of two glyph-pairs. The first five of these are generally the cycle glyphs and numbers that describe the position in the 13-baktun cycle when the stela was erected. Usually read from left to right and top to bottom, in most cases the glyph-pairs are followed by the number and glyph of the relevant Tzolkin day. Then come two glyphs relating to the relevant Night Lord—first the name of the ruling Night Lord, and next, it is thought, the title, "Night Lord."

After these come a series of lunar glyphs describing the relevant moon age (or phase), the position of the lunar month in the lunar half-year, the name of the lunation (and a glyph meaning "it is named"), and then a glyph signifying whether the lunation is of 29 or 30 days. Finally, there is a glyph-pair that describes the Haab date. An example of a stela from Quirigua is shown (*opposite*).

The next group of glyphs was originally called the Secondary Series, but they are now called "distance-number" dates. They are shorthand date calculations—counts of days to be added or subtracted from the "base date" or full Long Count date on the monument. They can record further dates as little as a day from the base date, or millions of years from it, and were often used by Maya lords to connect with their ancestry, legitimizing their rulership.

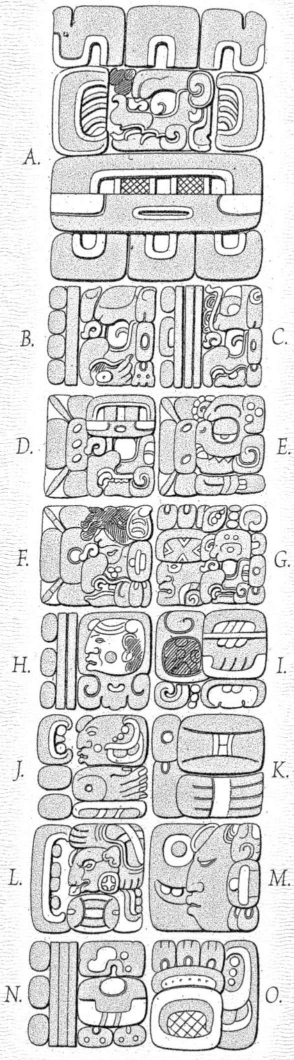

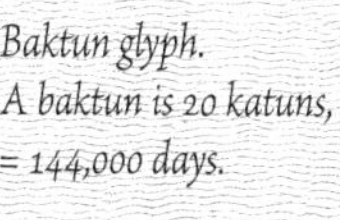

Baktun glyph.
A baktun is 20 katuns,
= 144,000 days.

Katun glyph.
A katun is 20 tuns,
= 7,200 days.

Tun glyph.
A tun is 18 uinals,
= 360 days.

Uinal glyph.
A uinal is 20 kin,
= 20 days.

Kin glyph.
A kin is
1 day.

Above: The repeating 20-fold structure of the Long Count.

Left: Long Count example from top half of Monument 6, Quirigua, Guatemala, showing the same date as the mechanism on the previous page.
A: Long Count Introducing Glyph. The head in the center is the patron deity of the Haab month, in this case Cumku. B: 9 baktuns. C: 17 katuns. D: 0 tuns. E: 0 uinals. F: 0 kins. G. Night Lord 9 & Gods of the Underworld glyph.
H: Tzolkin date. 13 Ahau. I: Lunar phase, here a new moon. J: Moon position (month), 2 within lunar half-year. K: Name of the current moon.
L: " ... is his [the moon's] princely name."
M: Current lunar month, here 29 days.
N: Haab date, here 18 Cumku. O: "he ... [verb]."

The Solar Zenith

tubes and alignments

The dates for sowing and harvesting were, and still are, fixed by the Maya at the two annual *zenith passage* days of the sun, when the sun is directly overhead, when a *gnomon* casts no shadow at noon. At some Mesoamerican sites, such as Xochicalco and Monte Alban, there are buildings in which a zenith tube projects a vertical sunbeam onto the floor at midday (*below*). In the Yucatan, bottle-shaped underground chambers called *chultunes* may have served the same purpose.

There are two seasons—rainy and dry, starting in April/May and November. The onset of the rainy season coincides with the first zenith passage in May for much of the Maya area, and maize (corn) is planted shortly after. At the second solar passage a second maize crop is planted. At higher altitudes, maize and beans are planted in March and harvested 260 days later in December.

The solar nadir dates (when the sun passes directly underfoot) are spaced six months from the zenith passage dates and the November solar nadir coincides with the beginning of the dry season.

Zenith tubes may also have been used to observe the zenith passage of important constellations. There is evidence suggesting the Aztecs interpreted the conjunction of the Pleiades with the zenith sun as a signal for the end of one era and the start of the next.

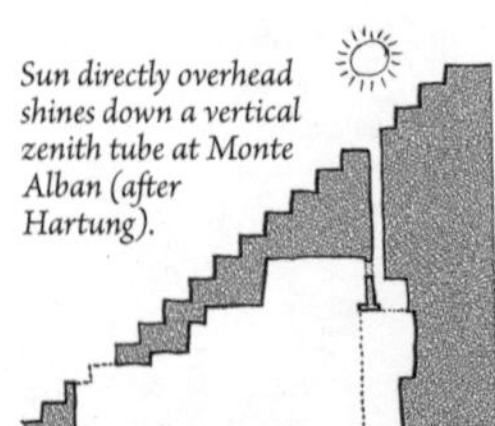

Sun directly overhead shines down a vertical zenith tube at Monte Alban (after Hartung).

The Central Mexican year-sign may represent an instrument that projects a cross on the zenith passage days (after Jenkins).

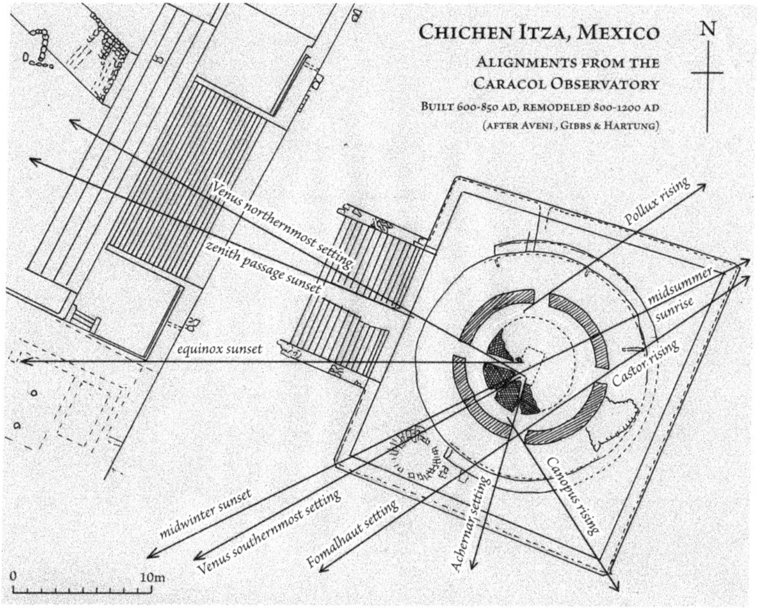

Chichen Itza, Mexico

Alignments from the Caracol Observatory

Built 600-850 AD, remodeled 800-1200 AD

(after Aveni, Gibbs & Hartung)

N

Venus northernmost setting

zenith passage sunset

Pollux rising

midsummer sunrise

equinox sunset

Castor rising

midwinter sunset

Venus southernmost setting

Fomalhaut setting

Achernar setting

Canopus rising

0 10m

The solar year, equinoxes, and solstices were determined by alignments, as here at Chichen Itza.

The Aztec Sunstone

a fossilized chronometer

In 1790, while installing water pipes in Mexico City's Central Plaza, laborers unearthed a huge carved stone disk, 2 feet thick and 12 feet in diameter, weighing 24 metric tons. Now on display in the National Museum of Anthropology in Mexico City, the disk is known as the Aztec Sunstone or Calendar Stone.

The Aztecs inherited their calendar from the Toltecs, contemporary with the later Maya, and it clearly shares similar origins. The 13 Reed glyph at the top of the stone is thought to refer to year 13 Reed, 1479, when the calendar stone may have been made. Surrounding the central panel is a ring showing the 20 day-signs, depicted differently from the 20 Maya signs.

The central panel may show the five gods that represent the five ages of the world, called the "Suns." Four rectangular motifs show the four previous Suns, while the central circle shows the face of Tonatiuh (or Huitzilpochtli), the Sun god who rules the present era, the "fifth and final Sun" (though the Aztecs had no Long Count).

In the analysis opposite, the underlying geometry of the various rings has been used to suggest a new interpretation. For instance, Ring E (*opposite*) has 56 elements, some hidden. The same number appears at Stonehenge, and is useful for eclipse prediction.

In a theoretical (Antikythera-style) version with moving parts the 20 day-signs could combine both with the 13 positions on the outer rim (to produce the Tzolkin), and with the mostly hidden Ring B of 18 quincunxes (to give a series of 18 20-day uinals). In this way, an original model could have tracked solstices, lunar nodes, eclipses, the Venus Round, the Tzolkin and the Long Count of the Maya.

A. Tonatiuh, Sun God. B. 18 Uinals (2 showing).
C. Four Catastrophic Era-Endings. D. 20 Day-Signs. E. 56 Eclipse Markers.
F. 104 Feathers, two Calendar Rounds, one Venus Round. G. Eight Solar Rays.
H. 96 Teeth, a quarter of 13 full moons. I. The Year 13 Reed.
J. 26 Snake Segments. K. Dark and Light Gods in Galactic Serpent's Mouth.

Galactic Alignment

to the stars and beyond

As more became known about the Mayan calendars, people began to wonder what the Maya might have been tracking with the Long Count. Recent research by John Major Jenkins suggests that they were actually measuring precession—using winter solstice sunrise. In particular, instead of focusing their cycle on its beginning, they targeted it on its end-point, which, according to the most popular correlation between Maya and Gregorian calendars (*see appendix p.57*) is an important winter solstice when the apparent center of the galaxy also lines up. Jenkins assembled a huge collection of evidence from Maya mythology and iconography to support his theory.

At the Pre-Classic Maya site of Izapa, where the Long Count was probably invented, various monuments show scenes that recall the Maya creation myth, the *Popol vuh*. The story describes the journey of the "hero twins" into the underworld to try to resurrect their father, the solar/maize deity One Hunahpu, by shaking the current ruler, Seven Macaw, off his perch. Seven Macaw is the Maya name for the Big Dipper constellation, and precession moved it from its perch (the rotational pole of the earth) between 1500 and 1000 BC.

One 26,000-tun cycle (25,627 years) of precession is five 13-baktun cycle eras (suns) of 5,200 tuns (5125 years) each. At the end of the current 13-baktun cycle, at winter solstice in 2012, the midwinter sun will align with the dark rift of the Milky Way, which the Maya called *xibalba be*, the black road that leads to the underworld.

This was depicted as the rebirth of the sun in the mouth of a crocodile or jaguar-toad, and also in the Mayan ballgame, where the ball going through the goal-ring represented the galactic alignment.

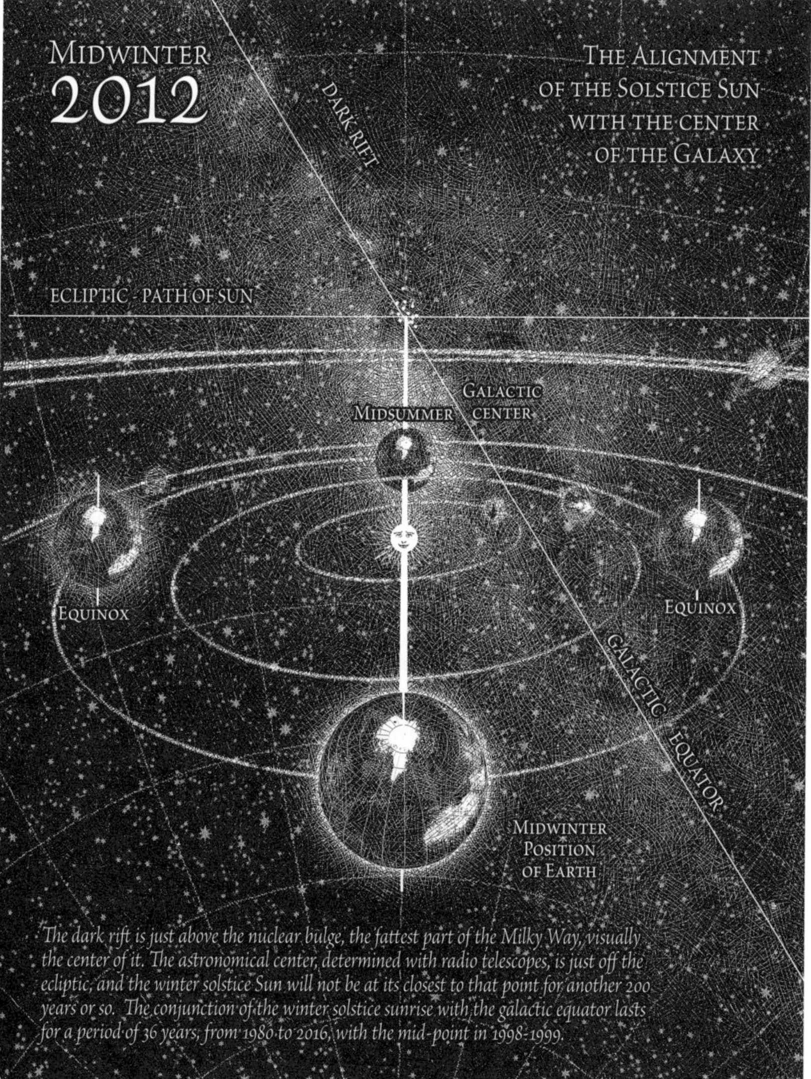
MIDWINTER
2012
THE ALIGNMENT
OF THE SOLSTICE SUN
WITH THE CENTER
OF THE GALAXY
DARK RIFT
ECLIPTIC - PATH OF SUN
GALACTIC
MIDSUMMER
CENTER
EQUINOX
EQUINOX
GALACTIC
EQUATOR
MIDWINTER
POSITION
OF EARTH
The dark rift is just above the nuclear bulge, the fattest part of the Milky Way, visually the center of it. The astronomical center, determined with radio telescopes, is just off the ecliptic, and the winter solstice Sun will not be at its closest to that point for another 200 years or so. The conjunction of the winter solstice sunrise with the galactic equator lasts for a period of 36 years, from 1980 to 2016, with the mid-point in 1998-1999.

2012 - End of Time

birth of the new sun

The Classic Maya site of Tortuguero is situated on the northernmost slopes of the Chiapas highlands in Mexico. Scholars have known since the 1970s that Monument 6, (originally T-shaped and covered with inscriptions), mentions the end-point of the 13-baktun cycle, due in 2012 AD, and is the only Maya inscription found to do so.

The left "wing" of the monument is missing, the central section partly effaced, and the part where the prophecy is recorded has a big crack through it, making a full translation virtually impossible. However, in April 2006, epigrapher Dave Stuart of the University of Texas offered a tantalizing fresh translation (*opposite*).

In this book, we have followed mankind's struggles to understand and map astronomical cycles from the dawn of history. Amazingly, the Maya exceeded the accuracy of all previous attempts, predicting the position of moon, planets, and eclipses far into the future. Their calendar was also imbued with divinatory and prophetic powers. They foresaw collapse, loss, plagues, famine, invasion, and the end of the priesthood for katun 13 Ahau, when the Spanish arrived.

The clock currently reads katun 4 Ahau, when the *Chilam Balam* predicted the return of Kukulcan. Katun 4 Ahau is also "the katun for remembering knowledge and compressing it within annals." This book has attempted to do exactly that. Hopefully, it will preserve the fascinating calendrical knowledge of the Maya and other ancient timekeepers well beyond 2012.

Left: An idealized stela showing the full 2012 Long Count end date. In the archeological example below the date is in the form of a period-ending date where only the baktun and the Tzolkin and Haab dates are shown.

Below: Monument 6 from Tortuguero, Mexico, which contains a prophecy regarding the 2012 end date. The text reads as: "Tzuhtz-(a)j-oom u(y)-uxlajuun pik; (ta) Chan Ajaw ux(-te') Uniiw. Uht-oom ? Y-em(al)?? Bolon Yookte' K'uh ta ?" which Stuart translates as "The Thirteenth Bak'tun will be finished (on) 4 Ahaw, the 3rd of K'ank'in ... ? will occur. (It will be) the descent(?) of the Nine Support (?) God(s) to the (?)..."

Right (continued): Question marks refer to damaged sections of the text. The top right glyphs are clearly identfiable as 13 baktuns, 4 Ahau, 3 Kankin, the 2012 end date. The Nine Gods in question are mentioned in the Chilam Balam books, as is the suggestion that the gods will return at the end of the 13-katun cycle, or Short Count. However, the translator, Maud Makemson, found evidence in the Tizimin that the prophecies originally applied to the end of the 13-baktun cycle, but were re-applied to the shorter cycle when the Long Count fell out of use (see The Books of Chilam Balam, appendices p.56).

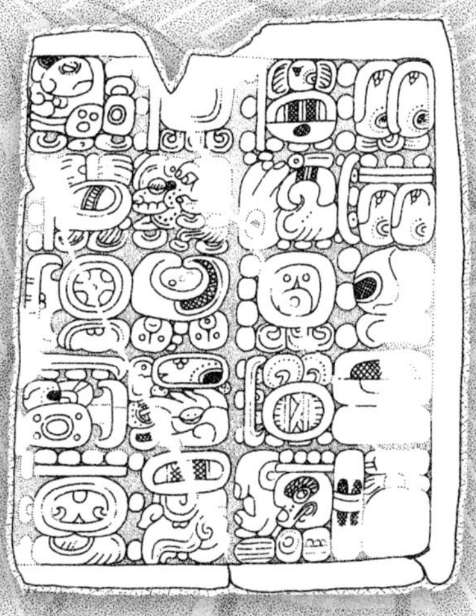

GLOSSARY OF ITALICIZED TERMS

819-day cycle: Mayan. Combines the 7 Earth gods, 9 Underworld gods (Night Lord cycle) and 13 Heaven gods into a cycle that tracks Jupiter and Saturn. Its start point has been traced back (by Thompson) to a day that is three days before the Day of Creation in 3114 BC.

Calendar Round: Mayan. The time taken for a given Tzolkin day to re-combine with a given Haab day. This was 52 haabs (13 days less than 52 solar years) or 73 tzolkins. It was a time of much celebration, when the New Fire Ceremony was held and the position of the Pleiades in the sky was noted.

Callipic cycle: Suggested in 325 BC by the Greek philosopher Callipus, it consists of 4 Metonic cycles with the 940 lunar months having 29 or 30 days each to give a total of 27,759 days.

Codex: An important manuscript or volume. The Maya codices are made from the inner bark of trees, which is folded into a long strip and folded like a screen, and covered with white lime, on which brightly colored glyphs and pictures are painted on both sides.

Codices: *see Codex*

Cross-quarter: A day falling approximately halfway between a solstice and an equinox, celebrated as pagan festivals.

Decan: The Egyptians used the heliacal rising of 36 stars or decans to mark the passage of their 10-day "weeks," of which there were three per month. The stars also marked the passage of "hours" of the night (varying length depending on season). When the zodiac was adopted in the Hellenistic period, the decans were adapted to three per zodiac sign.

Draconic Year: See Eclipse Year

Eclipse Year: The length of time it takes for the sun to return to the same lunar node. For an eclipse of any kind to occur both sun and moon must be at or very close to one or other of the moon's nodes.

Ecliptic: The extension of the earth's orbit onto the stars, the circle around earth which is the passage of the sun.

Epagomenal: These five days were holidays and commemorated the birthdays of the gods Osiris, Isis, Horus, Nephthys and Seth - the epagomenal neters (gods) who were born on the 5 extra days outside the 12 30-day months.

Equinox: The days halfway between solstices, when the day and night are of equal length, around 21 March and 22 September. An amazing equinox marker was built in the form of the Pyramid of Kukulcan at Chichen Itza, which gives the illusion of a huge snake descending and ascending the pyramid at the equinoxes.

Great Year: One full cycle of the *precession of the equinoxes*. Values vary: 25,920 years (Platonic Year), 25,627 years (Mayan value), 25,772 years (modern value).

Great Month: One twelfth of a great year. Denoted by the zodiacal sign currently behind the sun at spring equinox. The months, decans, (and time itself according to the Copts) seem to run backwards (*precession*), bulls become calves, rams become lambs.

Gregorian calendar: Named after Pope Gregory XIII, and devised by Aloysius Lillius, this is the calendar reform instituted in Spain, Portugal and Italy in 1582, that added an extra leap-year rule and deleted 10 days, so 4 Oct 1582 was followed by 15 Oct. The previous Julian calendar simply had one leap-year every 4 years, while the Gregorian rule was that a leap-year must be divisible by 4, unless it is divisible by 100 - then it is not a leap-year - unless it is divisible by 400, in which case it is a leap-year. In Denmark, Norway and Protestant Germany 18th Feb 1700 was followed by 1 March. The British Empire (including the US) did not adopt the Gregorian calendar until 1752, by which time it was necessary to delete 11 days. In Russia 31 Jan 1918 was followed by 14 Feb.

Heliacal rising: Of a star, moon or planet. When it first becomes visible above the Eastern horizon at dawn, after being hidden below the horizon or in the glare of the sun.

Intercalation: The insertion of a leap-day, -week or -month into a calendar to follow the seasons or lunar phases.

Julian calendar: Introduced in 46 BC by Julius Caesar. It consisted of 12 months of the same lengths as we have in the Gregorian calendar, making a 365-day year to which a leap-day was added every 4 years. It is accurate to 1 day in 128 years, and had dropped behind the solar year by 10 days by the time of the Gregorian calendar reform of 1582.

Leap: An extra day, week or month added into a calendar to keep it in time with seasons or lunar phases

Lunar Year. Normally the period taken for 12 lunations.

Lunation: The period betwen new (or full) moons. Equal on average to 29.53059 days

Mayan: The adjectival form of Maya. In recent years the protocol amongst Mayanists has been to use Maya for everything except for the language (Mayan). In this book we have followed the more common usage.

Metonic cycle: A cycle discovered by the Greek astronomer, Meton 432 BC, that was useful for harmonizing the solar and lunar cycles. After 19 solar years, 235 lunations occur, and the same lunar phase re-occurs on the same solar calendar date as 19 solar years previously. It appears earlier in British neolithic sites from 2500 BC and in the Chinese calendar from 1500 BC.

Moon's Nodes: Where the sun's and moon's paths cross.

Nilometer. A device for measuring the water level of the river Nile, which determined the timing of the annual flood. The devices were inscribed columns or steps going into the water, or in some cases, a channel that led into a cistern

Platonic Year. See Great Year.

Precession of the equinoxes: The earth's tilt slowly spins in space like a wobbly spinning-top. This means that the zodiacal stars behind the equinoctial (and solsticial) sun are slowly shifting backwards.

Retrograde: Planets occasionally appear to go backwards across the stars when seen from Earth.

Saros: An 18-year cycle of eclipses. Eclipses of similar types and duration recur shifted slightly north or south after 18 years, 11 days, and 8 hours.

Season: Meteorological (weather and temperate) cycle, normally connected with the tropical year.

Sidereal: In relation to the stars. A sidereal day is the time taken for one 360^{0} rotation of the Earth, when a star can again be observed in the same position (e.g., directly overhead). It is shorter than a solar or tropical day (there are 366.2422 sidereal days per tropical year). The sidereal year is 20 minutes and 24 seconds longer than the tropical year, and consists of exactly one more sidereal day (366.25636042 sidereal or 365.25636042 mean solar days).

Solstice: The point at which the plane of the Earth's axial tilt crosses the sun. At these times the sun reaches its annual stand-still points on the horizon at sunrise and sunset - producing its most northerly and southerly risings and settings. The summer solstice is around 21 June and the winter solstice is around 21 December.

Sothic: The Sothic calendar (civil calendar or Canicular period), was named after Sothis - the Greek name for Sirius - and had no leap-day, so the year drifted through the seasons, slipping back a day every four years, taking 1461 *vague* or Egyptian years (of 365 days) before New Year again realigned with the rising of Sirius (so 1461 vague or Egyptian years = 1460 Julian 365.25-day years). This period is known as the Sothic cycle.

Synodic: The synodic year of a planet is the time it takes to reappear at the same point in the sky relative to the sun (as observed from Earth). Typically it may be imagined as the interval between superior conjuctions of the planet with the sun (where the planet passes behind the sun).

Tropical: In relation to the seasons. Typically, a tropical, or solar, year is the time taken between any given solstice or equinox. The time will vary slightly according to whichever one chooses - the average of all possible points is called the mean tropical year.

Trecena: The Spanish term used to identify the 13-day period or "week" that was being used by the Aztecs. The term is also now used to refer to the same cycle in the Maya Tzolkin, although they did not term it such.

Vague year. A year of 365 days with no leap-year days added, such as the Egyptian year and the Haab of the Maya.

Venus round: Mayan. The time taken for a given Tzolkin day and given Haab day to re-combine with a given phase of Venus. 2 Calendar Rounds or 104 haabs (146 tzolkins), 65 584-day Venus cycles, or 13 Venus pentagrams.

Year-drift formula: At Palenque two date inscriptions show an interval of 1508 haabs (29 Calendar Rounds), equivalent to 1507 solar years (accurate to four decimal places). Mayanists call this the "year-drift formula." The *Dresden Codex* demonstrates that in Early Post-Classic times the months of the Haab still drifted through the solar year, but according to Milbrath, there is evidence that in the Late Post-Classic period, the festival calendar of the Yucatec Maya became locked to the solar year by the intercalation of leap days. Thompson says this did not happen until the year 1553 (over 30 years after the end of the Post-Classic).

Zodiac: A set of constellations along the ecliptic through which the sun travels every year. The one used by Indo-European cultures was developed in Babylon in the first millennium BC and consists of 12 signs. The Chinese zodiac also has 12 signs, but the Maya are thought to have used a 13-sign zodiac.

ADDENDA - ADDITIONAL CALENDRICAL NOTES

AZTEC: [*see too p. 44*]. On the Aztec Sunstone, the five central gods are enclosed in the Ollin glyph, the day-sign of movement or earthquake. The four gods surrounding Tonatiuh (the sun god) are also day-signs in the 260-day calendar, and are each accompanied by four circular "buttons," possibly the dates on which the previous Suns ended – 4 Ocelot, 4 Wind, 4 Rain and 4 Water. These glyphs may represent the type of disaster that ended those Suns - people being eaten (representing an eclipse according to Brotherston); hurricanes; rains of molten lava; and flooding. Although the central deity is a Sun-god, the current era could end in an earthquake, rather than any solar effects due to Tonatiuh, because Ollin encapsulates the five eras. However, various authorities have explained Ollin as the 4 motions of the Sun, or 4 previous world ages, encapsulating all the eras. Also, since the four glyphs are in different year-bearer groups, they cannot be year-bearers in the 52-year Calendar Round. Maybe a re-interpretation is in order. Brotherston found 100 Calendar Rounds (5200 years) encoded on the rim of the Sunstone. Could they be a dim memory of the 5200-tun Long Count of the Maya?

CHINESE: [*see too p.6*]. The reformed intercalation system says that if there are thirteen new moons (or twelve unbroken moons) from the start of the 11th month (containing the Winter Solstice) to the start of the 11th month the next year then an extra month must be inserted at the end of the first (there is normally only one) month during which two full moons both occupy the same zodiacal sign. The Chinese luni-solar calendar also has 24 divisions called Solar Terms, based on the longitude of the Sun on the ecliptic, and named after the four quarters and the weather, e.g., *Spring Begins*; *Summer Solstice*; *Great Heat*; and *White Dew*. Most are 15 days in length, but six are 16 days, and one is 14 days (total: 365). Each zodiac sign relates to two Solar Terms, with four of the signs overlapping two seasons.

EGYPTIAN [*see p. 12*]: The Egyptians were using the 1460-year Sothic cycle. Since Censorius records that the Egyptian New Year and the heliacal rising of Sirius coincided in 139AD, the calendar probably started in 2782 BC, but some historians have pushed the start back a further 1460 years to around 4242 BC (Egyptologist J.H. Breasted says 4236 BC). Each month was divided into three weeks of ten days each, making 36 weeks in the year. The day and night were each divided into twelve equal parts, the lengths of which varied according to the time of year, and were tracked with sundials, the shadows of obelisks, and water clocks. There were three seasons based around the Nile flooding – Inundation, Planting and Harvesting, each four months in length. A new lunar calendar was introduced for religious festivals. Originally, this had a month intercalated every time the first day of the lunar year came before the first day of the civil calendar, but this was replaced by a 25-year cycle of intercalation, equal to 309 lunations. In 238 BC, Ptolemy III tried to introduce a leap day, but the priests ignored him. It was eventually implemented in 25 BC by Caesar Augustus.

HEBREW / BABYLONIAN: The Hebrew calendar is a very ancient luni-solar one. It consists of 12 lunar months of alternating 29 and 30 days, though months 8 and 9 sometimes break this rule. To keep Passover in Spring, an intercalary month was inserted if the barley hadn't yet ripened. After the Babylonian exile (586 BC), the Jews adopted Babylonian names for their months and the Metonic method of intercalation. In the Babylonian Metonic system a 30-day month was added after Addaru, in years 3, 6, 8, 11,14 and 19, and a 29-day month was added after Ululu in year 17. In the Jewish version, the extra month (Adar I) was inserted between the 11th and 12th months (Shevat and Adar) (the 12th, now 13th, month was renamed Adar II). In Babylon there were 12 months each year, plus an extra month added 7 times over 19 years, totalling 6939 days, but, in the Jewish version, depending on the day of the week that Rosh Hashanah (New Year, Sept 5th - Oct 5th) falls on, and the length of the year, months 8 and 9 sometimes vary from their normal length. The result is a 19-year cycle that varies between 6939 and 6942 days, made up of years that vary in length from 353-355 days (or 383-385 days in leap years). The Hebrew calendar has a mean error of 1 day in 224 years., while the Babylonian version was a day off every 219 years.

INUIT: The Inuit people of Northern Canada have a polar night, in which the Sun does not rise for 4 and a half months. Dawn and twilight each last for about 3 weeks, and daylight reigns for the remaining 6 months. The Moon rises and sets once per month. When risen, its light reflects off the snow, which, combined with snow storms, clouds and the aurora borealis, means the stars are only visible for about 2 months per year. The Inuit use a 13-month lunar calendar, the year beginning when the Sun reappears on the horizon after the polar night - this is at a different time for different Inuit groups, depending on their latitude, but the event was signaled by the rising of the stars Altair and Tarazed. They have 16 constellations, but do not seem to recognize the North Star.

ISLAMIC: The Islamic or Hijri calendar is fully lunar. There are twelve months of 29 or 30 days, with the first day of each month set by the first sighting of the crescent moon. To keep up with the moon, 11 days are added every 30 years, in years 2, 5, 7, 10, 13, 16, 18, 21, 24, 26, and 29. In leap years, the extra day is added to the 12th month, so it has 30 days instead of 29. It is accurate to one day in 3320 years. The second Caliph Umar instituted the modern calendar from the time of the Prophet Muhammad's prohibition of intercalary months. The first day of the first month of the first Islamic year corresponds to July 16, 622 AD. For a rough conversion, the Christian AD year = the Islamic year AH x 0.97.

PLAYING CARDS: A pack of playing cards contains a calendar. Four seasons of 1+2+3+4+5+6+7+8+9+10+11+12+13 = 91 days each is 364 days. Plus a joker gives 365.

TIBETAN: The Tibetans have a luni-solar calendar in which there are usually 12 months that begin and end on the new crescent moon. A 13th month is added every 3 years or so: The year is divided into 24, and the even-numbered divisions (zhong-qi) are examined. If no zhong-qi falls unbroken in a lunar month, it becomes a leap-month. To compute the length of the month, a "lunar day" is used (time to travel 12 degrees); if the ends of two lunar days fall on one solar day, then a day is skipped; if no lunar day ends on a solar day, a day is added. All months are either 29 or 30 days. The New Year celebration is called Losar, on the 1st day of the first month (around February). Like China, Tibet names its years after one of 12 animals and one of 5 elements, producing a 60-year *Rab-byung* cycle. Another calendar, the *Kalachakra*, is a 12-month solar calendar governed by the Sun's path through the 12 sidereal zodiac signs (currently shifted 24° forwards from the Western tropical zodiac). The Kalachakra New Year (0° Aries) is currently 12th April. The Elemental New Year occurs on the 1st day of the new moon of the 11th lunar month, which is always a Tiger month (around December).

Table of Ordered Month Names

for naming purposes only, solar calendrical dates do not line up horizontally.

Name	Chinese	Egyptian	Babylonian	Hebrew	Islamic	Julian
Date	2600 BC	1800 BC	2000 BC	580 BC	622 AD	46 BC
Type	Lunar 29-30 days	30-day months	Lunar	Lunar	Lunar 29 or 30 days	Solar
New Year	2nd new moon	1 Thoth	1st new moon	Sept 5th	1 Muharram	1 January
w.r.t. Solar	after winter solstice	Movable	after Spring Eq.	to Oct 5th	Movable	always
1	First (29/30)	Thoth	Nisanu (30)	Nisan (30)	Muharram (29/30)	January (31)
2	Apricot (29/30)	Phaophi	Ayaru (29)	Iyar (29)	Safar (29/30)	February (28/29)
3	Peach (29/30)	Athyr	Simanu (30)	Sivan (30)	Rabi' al-awwal (29/30)	March (31)
4	Mei (29/30)	Choak	Du'uzu (29)	Tammuz (29)	Rabi' al-thani (29/30)	April (30)
5	Pomegranate (29/30)	Tybi	Abu (30)	Av (30)	Jumada al-awwal (29/30)	May (31)
6	Lotus (29/30)	Mechir	Ululu (29)	Elul (29)	Jumada al-thani (29/30)	June (30)
7	Orchid (29/30)	Phamenoth	Tashritu (30)	Tishrei (30)	Rajab (29/30)	July (31)
8	Osmanthus (29/30)	Pharmouthi	Arakhsamna (29)	Cheshvan (29/30)	Sha'aban (29/30)	August (31)
9	Chrysanthemum (29/30)	Pachon	Kislimu (30)	Kislev (30/29)	Ramadan (29/30)	September (30)
10	Good (29/30)	Payni	Tebetu (29)	Tevet (29)	Shawwal (29/30)	October (31)
11	Hiemal (29/30)	Epiphi	Shabatu (30)	Shevat (30)	Dhu al-Qi'dah (29/30)	November (30)
12	Last (29/30)	Mesore	Adaru (29)	Adar (30)	Dhu al-Hijjah (29/30)	December (31)
Leap Month	Thirteenth (29/30)	-	Adaru II (30) Ululu II (29)	Adar II (29)	-	-

Popol Vuh - The Five Eras

The *Popol vuh*, or "Book of the Mat" is a long mythological poem of the Quiche Maya, from the highlands of Guatemala. Written in Utatlan in the 16th century from a combination of oral and written sources, it has some Spanish influence, and tells a Mayan creation myth, in which, according to Brotherston, four previous ages are described. First is the age of mud people, who are returned to water. Second is the age of the doll people, who are consumed by monsters during an eclipse. The third (some say the current) age is of Seven Macaw, defeated by the Hero Twins. Fourth is the descent to Xibalba, when the Hero Twins ascend to the sky. Fifth is the current era, when the Maize people – the Quiche – are created. However, some interpreters find only three or four ages described in the *Popol vuh*.

The *Murals of the Four Suns*, at Tonina and Palenque, show four upside-down heads and an overseeing skull (representing the Suns reborn at each Creation) and a skull-like head wearing a necklace of four tassels (stylized heads with hair hanging down). These are reminiscent of the five ages depicted at the center of the Aztec Sunsone (and described in the *Cuautitlan Annals*) – a central skull with four surrounding eras.

Martín Prechtel has described the Creation myths of the Tzutujil Maya as five eras of fire, plants, water, wind, and movement, very similar to the Aztec ones: water/flood; wind; fire/rain of fire; starvation/eaten by jaguars/eclipse; movement/earthquake. Instead of being focused on the destruction of the ages, like the Aztec versions, the Tzutujil version describes an evolution of souls through these phases in continuing incarnations. The current world is also called the Earth Fruit World, as humans reach their full potential.

The Aztec versions suggest various lengths of time for the eras. One source, the *Leyenda del Sols*, gives different lengths, which are all multiples of the 52-year Calendar Round. But five of the 5,200-tun Mayan 13-baktun cycle eras add to 26,000 tuns – the precession of the equinoxes, which is surely significant.

Origins of the Mayan Calendar

According to some Maya scholars, the calendrical and writing systems used by the Maya began with the Zapotecs (near Oaxaca, in Mexico), around 600 BC, since the earliest calendrical glyphs have been found at Monte Alban, (founded between 700 BC and 500 BC). However, others argue that the Tzolkin must have been previously developed elsewhere. Malmstrom suggests it was developed by the Olmecs at Izapa in 1359 BC, that the Haab originated there in 1376 BC and the Long Count in 236 BC, though some argue the Tzolkin is older than the Haab. Justeson says it has been recorded as early as 900-700 BC by the Olmecs.

Some put the start of the Long Count at 550 BC – others say around 355 BC, but most Mayanists would say the first century BC, or just before, as the oldest recorded Long Count date is 7.16.3.2.13, 6th December 36 BC, from Chiapa de Corzo, inhabited by descendants of the Olmecs. The oldest discovered Maya date – 292 AD – is on Stela 29 at Tikal.

Bricker estimates that the Haab was first used around 550 BC with the starting point of the Winter Solstice. Edmonson says there is evidence for the Calendar Round among the Olmecs in 667 BC. The Olmec civilization started between 1800 and 1200 BC according to various sources, and they settled in Izapa from 1500 BC or between 800 and 500 BC (sources vary). Izapa is on a latitude that results in periods of 260 days and 105 days between zenith passages of the Sun, which suggests that this town may indeed have been the origin-point of the Tzolkin.

a.

Some Incredible Dates

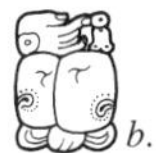
b.

There are several inscriptions that show colossal time calculations, in terms of pictuns (*a.*) (20 baktuns or 8,000 tuns); calabtuns (*b.*) (20 pictuns or 160,000 tuns); kinchiltuns (20 calabtuns or 3,200,000 tuns); and alautuns (20 kinchiltuns or 64,000,000 tuns). Some of these inscriptions include occasional mistakes, which has made decoding them difficult, but Thompson has managed it. Most of these are in the form of distance dates, where a Long Count date is given, such as this one on Tikal stela 10: 9.8.9.13.0 8 Ahau 13 Pop, (24th March 603 AD Gregorian), with the distance date 10.11.10.5.8 to be added. The resulting date is given as 1.0.0.0.0.8 5 Lamat 1 Mol. Here, the pictun coefficient is given as 1. This is 21st October 4772 AD – a calculation of over 3000 years into the future.

Even more impressive, though, is the inscription on Quirigua stela F, or 6. Here the Long Count date reads 9.16.10.0.0 1 Ahau 3 Zip (15th March 761 AD Gregorian). The huge distance date of 1.8.13.0.9.16.10.0.0 is subtracted and the resulting date is given as (18.)13.0.0.0.0.0.0.0 1 Ahau 13 Yaxkin, which is equivalent to a day over 90 million years in the past. However, there is another distance date on Quirigua Stela D or 4, that gives a date of 9.16.15.0.0 7 Ahau 18 Pop (17th February 766 AD Gregorian), to which is added 6.8.13.0.9.16.15.0.0, to give a date of (13.)13.0.0.0.0.0.0.0. This is over 400 million years before the date the stela was erected! It was by calculating a number of these distance dates that Thompson was able to determine that the date of creation in 3114 BC – 13.0.0.0.0 was actually 0.1.13.0.0.0.0.0.0 in the extended version.

At Yaxchilan, on a temple stairway, a puzzling inscription includes four levels above the alautuns. It reads: 13.13.13.13.13.13.13.13.9.15.13.6.9 3 Muluc 17 Mac. This is equivalent to 19th October 744 AD, but as you can see, the higher cycles do not conform to Thompson's calculation. The same applies to Stela 1 at Coba, which shows a series of 24 cycles, when only 9 would be needed to chart the age of the universe!

c.

Period-Ending Dates

d.

Use of the full Long Count dating method was waning by the middle of the Late-Classic era, and started being replaced by the abbreviated period-ending dating (e.g., *c. & d. "end 13 baktuns"*). This system recorded only the name of the baktun (or later just the katun), and the calendar-round date – in other words, the baktun (or katun) plus the relevant Tzolkin and Haab days. This reduced the amount of glyphs necessary to record a date from ten to three, but it could still pinpoint dates in a 374,400- (or 19,000-) year window. By the time of the Late Post-Classic era, the system had been abbreviated even more. The katuns were now recorded not by their number as they would have been in the Long Count – the katun number in a series of the twenty in the baktun – but by the name of the Tzolkin day on which they ended. There are thirteen possible Tzolkin days on which the katuns ended – all Ahau. Thus, the cycle would repeat after thirteen katuns (256.27 solar years), so dates over a longer period could only be recorded if an entire series of these katun counts was listed.

Mayanists call this calendar the Short Count, since it consists of 13 katuns instead of 13 baktuns, and 260 tuns as opposed to the 260 katuns of the Long Count. Some Mayanists suppose that the sequence started on katun 8 Ahau and ended on katun 10 Ahau, since there is a series of prophecies starting and ending with those katuns in the *Chilam Balam* of Mani. Others have proposed that the series started with katun 11 Ahau and ended with katun 13 Ahau, as implied by a 1566 diagram by zealous book-burner Bishop Landa.

Three Realms & the 819 Day Cycle

The Mayan universe consisted of three realms: the visible realm of earth and two invisible realms – the celestial realm above, and *Xibalba*, the underworld below. Xibalba was the domain of death, the portals to which were caves, though the road to the underworld, *xibalba be*, was located in the dark-rift of the Milky Way (because the underworld rotates above the earth at night). The celestial realm consisted of thirteen layers, each presided over by one of the *Oxlahuntiku*, the Thirteen Gods of the Upper World, who were considered both as a collective deity and as separate entities, and whose name glyphs may have been the same as the first thirteen head-numeral glyphs. The nine gods are said to have fought and defeated the thirteen gods. The *Bolontiku* presided over the nine layers of Xibalba and were also seen both as one and nine gods. Their names and influences in the Maya system are unknown, (the Aztec versions are known, though they don't seem to correspond to the Maya glyphs), but they are referred to as Night Lords 1-9.

The Books of Chilam Balam

The books of *Chilam Balam*, (Books of the Jaguar Priest) were named after Yucatan shaman-seers. The earliest of these writings of prophecy, myth and ritual date back to 1593. They were written in the Maya language, but in European characters, the Spanish having taught the Maya how to write in Roman script. Several versions of the text appeared in various towns around the Yucatan in post-conquest years. The most well-known, named after the towns where they were found, include the *Mani*, *Tizimin*, and *Chumayel* versions, and the *Codex Perez*, a compilation of extracts of lost versions (not to be confused with the *Paris Codex*, which was also called Codex Perez at first).

The most significant part is the "count of katuns" – the series of 13 katuns with accompanying prophecies, (which would be repeated at the end of katuns of the same name in subsequent cycles). The ends of katuns were feared, as were the ends of haabs (the 5 *Uayeb* or unlucky days, when people hid away), eclipses, and risings of Venus.

The *Tizimin* writings were compiled into a collection in 1752. Although the *Chumayel* was written after a complete conversion to Christianity, the *Tizimin* was written before that had happened. The *Tizimin* records that the Itza overlords, (before the Spanish invasion) who had taken on the roles of the priesthood, had not retained the knowledge of the original priesthood, knew nothing about the days and katuns of the Maya calendars, and did not even know the names of the gods to invoke them correctly. The *Chilam Balam* of Mani was collected together and translated into Spanish by Don Juan Pio Perez, and published in1843, but he admitted to leaving out parts that offended his Christian beliefs.

The Chilam Balams are a confusing muddle of calendrical information, tainted by Spanish insertions, and even have some 24-year katuns, but they still give a valuable insight the rituals and beliefs of the Maya, (such as the 65-day burner cycle).

An example of the evidence that some of the prophecies originally referred to the Long Count can be found on *Tizimin* p.16: *"In the final days of tying up the bundle of the thirteen katuns on 4 Ahau...these valleys of the Earth shall come to an end. For those katuns there shall be no priests, and no one who believes in his government without having doubts...I recount to you the words of the true gods, when they shall come."*

Interestingly, the Short Count did not end on a 4 Ahau day, but the 13-baktun cycle of the Long Count does indeed end on 4 Ahau on 21st December 2012.

CONVERTING MAYAN DATES TO GREGORIAN

TO FIND THE EQUIVALENT DATE in the Gregorian calendar, to any Maya date, a correlation constant is used. This is the Julian day number that corresponds to the Creation date in 3114 BC, that the Maya recorded as 13.0.0.0.0 4 Ahau 8 Cumku, but which is also called 0.0.0.0.0. The Julian day numbers start at day zero on 1st January 4713 BC in the Julian calendar. Back-calculating in the Gregorian calendar that we use today, this is equivalent to 24th November 4714 BC.

Throughout the 20th century, a variety of scholars have proposed various correlation constants so that Mayan dates can be rendered in the Gregorian calendar. These range from the Wilson correlation in which 0.0.0.0.0 is equivalent to Julian day number 438906, (31st July 3512 BC Gregorian), to the Weitzel correlation in which 0.0.0.0.0 is equivalent to Julian day number 774078, (3rd April 2594 BC Gregorian). Ideally, the correlation used should be supported by dates recorded in ceramics, dates inscribed on stelae and buildings, cross-referenced Moon and Venus information, dates recorded in the Late-Classic codices such as the *Dresden Codex*, de Landa's recorded dates, Aztec dates of the arrival of Cortez, the *Chilam Balam* and other post-conquest books, and the unbroken Tzolkin count still being used today in the Highlands of Guatemala.

In practice, there is no correlation that will agree with all these, but some have come much closer than others. Today, most Mayanists agree that the best correlation is the Goodman-Martinez-Thompson (GMT) correlation. Of the three possible start-dates in the range, the most popular is the 584283, and the next is the 584285. These would correspond to an equivalent Gregorian date for 0.0.0.0.0 as 11th August 3114 BC and 13th August 3114 BC – a difference of only two days. The 584283 correlation was originally proposed in 1897 by Joseph Goodman, and was unpopular until 1926, when it was confirmed by Juan Martinez Hernandez. In 1927, Eric Thompson applied lunar and Venus information to arrive at a two-day adjustment – the 584285 correlation, later confirmed by Floyd Lounsbury, who found evidence to support it by cross-referencing astronomical phenomena with those recorded in the *Dresden Codex*. In 1950, Thompson made a final re-examination of Goodman's work, combining it with all the latest findings, and settled on the 584283 correlation. Unlike the Lounsbury, or 584285 correlation, this one coincides with the unbroken Tzolkin count kept by the Quiche Maya who still live in the Highlands of Guatemala. It also terminates on a Winter Solstice.

Older sources give the start-year of the 13-baktun cycle as 3113 BC, which was calculated without allowing for the fact that the Gregorian calendar has no zero-year, since the BC/AD divide goes from 1 BC to 1 AD. More recently, the zero-year has been included to make counting easier across the divide, and so the start-year is now known as 3114 BC.

TO CONVERT A MAYAN DATE from an inscription into a Gregorian date, an estimate can be made that should be within a decade. The completion of 9 baktuns (9.0.0.0.0) occurred in 435 AD (9th December Gregorian) – this is the start of the baktun when most inscriptions were made. Here is an example: Stela D or 4 at Quirigua shows a Long Count date of 9.16.10.0.0 1 Ahau 3 Zip. First, the estimate: to 435, simply add 16 katuns of approximately 20 years, plus 10 tuns of approximately a year each, and we get 435 + 320 + 10 = approximately 765 AD. The actual date is 15th March 761 AD (Gregorian).

To calculate this more accurately, we must count how many days before or after the 9th baktun – in this case, 16 katuns (16 x 7,200) plus 10 tuns (3,600) = 118,800 days. Divide 118,800 by 365.2425 = 325.263352 years. Multiply the decimal places by 365 to get the number of days = 96 days. Then add 325 years and 96 days to 9th December 425 AD to get 15th March 761 AD Gregorian (after dividing the year by 4 to see if it is a leap year).

Calculating Your Mayan Day-Sign

[1] Find the "birth year number" (*below left*) and add 1 if born after 29th Feb in a leap year*. [2] Add the "month number" as follows (Jan *0*, Feb *31*, Mar *59*, Apr *90*, May *120*, Jun *151*, Jul *181*, Aug *212*, Sep *243*, Oct *13*, Nov *44*, Dec *74*). [3] Add the day of the month. [4] If the number is now greater than 260, then subtract 260. [5] Locate the number on the Tzolkin grid (*below right*). Example: 5th March 1964: 212 + 1 + 59 + 5 - 260 = 17 = 4 Caban.

QUALITIES: Imix (Imox): Alligator (water lily); + *friendly, lively*; – *secretive, insane.* **Ik** (Iq) ; Wind (wind), + *imaginative, confident* – *angry, dishonest.* **Akbal** (Aqbal): House (darkness/dawn); + *intellectual, sincere*; – *complains, adulterer.* **Kan** (Kat): Lizard (net); + *leader, organized*; – *boring, sex-addict.* **Chicchan** (Kan): Serpent (snake); + *honest, discerning*; – *volatile, jealous.* **Cimi** (Keme): Death; + *kind, political*; – *materialistic, killer.* **Manik** (Kej): Deer (hand); + *strong, leader*, – *interfering, bossy.* **Lamat** (Qanil): Rabbit (rabbit, Venus); + *genius, adventurous*; – *gossip, drunk.* **Muluc** (Toj) : Water (jade, rain); + *independent, longsuffering*; – *sickly, tyrant.* **Oc** (Tzi): Dog (dog); + *fearless, headstrong*; – *jealous, judgmental.* **Chuen** (batz): Monkey (monkey, ball of thread); + *wise, creative*; – *unaccommodating, unclean.* **Eb** (E): Grass (tooth, road); + *generous, non-conformist*; – *lazy, vagabond.* **Ben** (Aj): Reed (corn plant, cane); + *perceptive, passionate*; – *opinionated, glutton.* **Ix** (Ix): Ocelot (jaguar, earth); + *gifted, vigorous*; – *distant, heart-broken.* **Men** (Tzikin): Eagle (bird, eagle); + *intelligent, eloquent*; – *fearful, pessimistic.* **Cib** (Ajmak): Vulture (wax); + *wise, courageous*; – *irresponsible, thief.* **Caban** (Noj): Earthquake (earthquake, thought); + *discerning, analytical*, – *bossy, devious.* **Etznab** (Tijax): Knife (obsidian blade); + *active, intelligent*; – *forgetful, slanderous.* **Cauac** (Kawoq): Rain (thunder, storm); + *vivacious, independent*; – *obstinate, paranoid.* **Ahau** (Ajpu): Flower (lord, sun); + *courageous, romantic*; – *impulsive, vengeful.*

Year	No.	Year	No.	Year	No.
1910	249	1957	256	2004*	2
1911	94	1958	101	2005	108
1912*	199	1959	206	2006	213
1913	45	1960*	51	2007	58
1914	150	1961	157	2008*	163
1915	255	1962	2	2009	9
1916*	100	1963	107	2010	114
1917	206	1964*	212	2011	219
1918	51	1965	58	2012*	64
1919	156	1966	163	2013	170
1920*	1	1967	8	2014	15
1921	107	1968*	113	2015	120
1922	212	1969	219	2016*	225
1923	57	1970	64	2017	71
1924*	162	1971	169	2018	176
1925	8	1972*	14	2019	21
1926	113	1973	120	2020*	126
1927	218	1974	225	2021	232
1928*	63	1975	70	2022	77
1929	169	1976*	175	2023	182
1930	14	1977	21	2024*	27
1931	119	1978	126	2025	133
1932*	224	1979	231	2026	238
1933	70	1980*	76	2027	83
1934	175	1981	182	2028*	188
1935	20	1982	27	2029	34
1936*	125	1983	132	2030	139
1937	231	1984*	237	2031	244
1938	76	1985	83	2032*	89
1939	181	1986	188	2033	195
1940*	26	1987	33	2034	40
1941	132	1988*	138	2035	145
1942	237	1989	244	2036*	250
1943	82	1990	89	2037	96
1944*	187	1991	194	2038	201
1945	33	1992*	39	2039	46
1946	138	1993	145	2040*	151
1947	243	1994	250	2041	257
1948*	88	1995	95	2042	102
1949	194	1996*	200	2043	207
1950	39	1997	46	2044*	52
1951	144	1998	151	2045	158
1952*	249	1999	256	2046	3
1953	95	2000*	101	2047	108
1954	200	2001	207	2048*	213
1955	45	2002	52	2049	59
1956*	150	2003	157	2050	164

		20	40	60	80	100	120	140	160	180	200	220	240	
Imix	1	8	2	9	3	10	4	11	5	12	6	13	7	+1
Ik	2	9	3	10	4	11	5	12	6	13	7	1	8	+2
Akbal	3	10	4	11	5	12	6	13	7	1	8	2	9	+3
Kan	4	11	5	12	6	13	7	1	8	2	9	3	10	+
Chicchan	5	12	6	13	7	1	8	2	9	3	10	4	11	+
Cimi	6	13	7	1	8	2	9	3	10	4	11	5	12	+
Manik	7	1	8	2	9	3	10	4	11	5	12	6	13	+
Lamat	8	2	9	3	10	4	11	5	12	6	13	7	1	+
Muluc	9	3	10	4	11	5	12	6	13	7	1	8	2	+
Oc	10	4	11	5	12	6	13	7	1	8	2	9	3	+
Chuen	11	5	12	6	13	7	1	8	2	9	3	10	4	+
Eb	12	6	13	7	1	8	2	9	3	10	4	11	5	+
Ben	13	7	1	8	2	9	3	10	4	11	5	12	6	+
Ix	1	8	2	9	3	10	4	11	5	12	6	13	7	+
Men	2	9	3	10	4	11	5	12	6	13	7	1	8	
Cib	3	10	4	11	5	12	6	13	7	1	8	2	9	
Caban	4	11	5	12	6	13	7	1	8	2	9	3	10	-
Etznab	5	12	6	13	7	1	8	2	9	3	10	4	11	-
Cauac	6	13	7	1	8	2	9	3	10	4	11	5	12	-
Ahau	7	1	8	2	9	3	10	4	11	5	12	6	13	-